KETO CHAFFLE RECIPES COOKBOOK FOR BEGINNERS

100 Simple Mouth-Watering Ideas Quick & Easy Ketogenic Low-Carb Waffles To Lose Weight & Maximize Your Health On The Ketogenic Diet.

By Wanda L. Avila

TABLE OF CONTENT

KETO CHAFFLE RECIPES COOKBOOK FOR BEGINNERS 1
TABLE OF CONTENT 2
INTRODUCTIONS 5
   What is a chaffle? 5
   Do chaffles just taste like burnt eggs and cheese? 5
   What other types of chaffles can you make? 5
   How do you make a chaffle? 6
      Keto chaffle recipes 7
      1. CLASSIC Chaffle Recipe 8
      2. ALMOND flour chaffle 9
      3. CREAM Cheese Coconut Flour Chaffle 11
      4. CHEDDAR & Herb Chaffle 13
      5. GARLIC Bread Chaffle 14
      6. GRILLED Cheese Chaffle 16
      7. PARMESAN Garlic Keto Chaffles 18
      8. HOT Ham & Cheese Chaffles 20
      9. WHITE Bread Keto Chaffle 21
      10. WONDER Bread Chaffles 23
      11. DAIRY FREE KETO CHAFFLE 24
      12. SAVORY Chaffle 25
      13. DAIRY Free and Egg Free Chaffle Bread 26
      14. TRADITIONAL KETO LOW CARB CHAFFLE 27
      15. KETO CHAFFLE BREAKFAST SANDWICH 28
      16. SIMPLE Keto Chaffles 30
      17. BUFFALO CHICKEN CHAFFLE 31
      18. CHEDDAR Chive Chaffles 33
      19. LEMON Ricotta Poppyseed Chaffles 35
      20. CHOCOLATE Chip Vanilla Chaffles 36
      21. SWEET Chocolate Chaffle 37
      22. RASPBERRY ALMOND CHAFFLES 39
      23. CHOCOLATE Cupcake Chaffle 40
      24. CHOCOLATE Chip Chaffles 41
      25. MAPLE PECAN KETO CHAFFLES 42
      26. YOGURT CHAFFLES 44
      27. KETO GINGERBREAD CHAFFLE 45
      28. BLUEBERRY CHAFFLES 46
      29. PEANUT BUTTER CHAFFLE 47
      30. KETO CHAFFLE GLAZED DONUT 48

31. CHOCOLATE CHIP CHAFFLES 50
32. LEMON CAKE CHAFFLES 51
33. KETO OREO CHAFFLES 52
34. KETO PUMPKIN CHAFFLES 54
35. BLACKBERRIES AND CREAM CHAFFLE 56
36. KETO STRAWBERRY SHORTCAKE CHAFFLE 57
37. PUMPKIN CHOCOLATE CHIP CHAFFLES 59
38. CHOCOLATE CHIP CHAFFLE 60
39. BROWNIE CHOCOLATE CHAFFLE 62
40. COFFEE CAKE CHAFFLES 63
41. PUMPKIN PECAN CHAFFLE 64
42. KETO RED VELVET CHAFFLES 66
43. PEANUT BUTTER CHOCOLATE CHIP CHAFFLE 67
44. KETO CINNAMON ROLL CHAFFLES 68
45. KETO BANANA NUT CHAFFLES 70
46. KETO CREAM CHEESE MINI CHAFFLE WAFFLES 72
47. KETO EGGNOG CHAFFLE 73
48. COCONUT CHOCOLATE CHIP MACADAMIA NUT CHAFFLES 75
49. COCONUT CREAM CAKE CHAFFLE 76
50. BLUEBERRY Cinnamon Keto Chaffles 78
51. WAFFLE Cereal 80
52. Keto Eggnog Chaffles 82
53. KETO BLACK FOREST CHAFFLE 83
54. HAM & Cheddar Chaffles 85
55. Chaffles with Bacon 86
56. KETO PIZZA CHAFFLES 87
57. VINTAGE CHEESE & POPPY SEEDS BISCUITS 89
58. BROCCOLI and Cheese Chaffle 90
59. AVOCADO Toast Chaffle 91
60. BROCCOLI Cheddar Chaffle 92
61. LOW Carb Bagel Chaffle 93
62. BROWN Butter Blueberry-Bacon Waffles 94
63. KETO TACO CHAFFLE 96
64. CHICKEN Bacon Ranch Chaffle 97
65. JALAPENO Popper Chaffle 98
66. SPINACH and Artichoke Chicken Chaffle 100
67. KETO Buffalo Chicken Chaffles 101
68. BACON, EGG, AND CHEESE CHAFFLE 103
69. KETO CAPRESE CHAFFLE RECIPE 104
70. ARBY'S Chaffle 105
71. SAUSAGE STUFFED CHAFFLE 107

- 72. GARLIC Parmesan chaffle 107
- 73. CRUNCHY Savory Keto Zucchini Chaffles 109
- 74. BACON Jalapeno Keto Chaffle 110
- 75. SALMON CHAFFLE TACOS 112
- 76. BURGER BUN CHAFFLE 114
- 77. PULLED PORK WITH CHAFFLE BUN 115
- 78. CHICKEN CHEDDAR CHAFFLE SANDWICH 116
- 79. Keto Okonomiyaki Chaffle 118
- 80. KETO PHILLY CHEESESTEAK CHAFFLE SANDWICH 121
- 81. TURKEY BRIE CRANBERRY CHAFFLE SANDWICH 123
- 82. KETO CORNBREAD CHAFFLES 124
- 83. SHRIMP AND AVOCADO CHAFFLE SANDWICH 126
- 84. LOW CARB CREAM CHEESE CHAFFLES 128
- 85. BLT CHAFFLE RECIPE 129
- 86. BROCCOLI & Cheese Chaffles 130
- 87. KETO COPY CAT BLOOMING ONION CHAFFLE STICKS WITH DIP ... 132
- 88. CRISPY KETO CHAFFLE CHIPS 133
- 89. KETO FRIED PICKLES 134
- 90. KETO CHEESESTEAK CHAFFLE SANDWICH 136
- 91. CRISPY KETO JALAPENO POPPER CHAFFLE 138
- 92. PEPPERONI PIZZA CHAFFLES 139
- 93. Chaffle Pepperoni Pizzas 140
- 94. KETO CHAFFLE PULLED PORK SANDWICH WITH CREAMY COLESLAW 142
- 95. TEX-MEX CHAFFLES 144
- 96. ULTIMATE keto protein chaffle 146
- 97. KETO CHAFFLE CUBAN SANDWICH 147
- 98. GARLIC and Herb Chaffle 150
- 99. KETO Belgian Chaffles 152
- 100. KETO Nutter Butter Chaffle 153

THE END 155

INTRODUCTIONS

What is a chaffle?

A chaffle is nothing more than an egg and cheese waffle. Before you turn away in disgust, let me assure you that this dish is excellent and that you will have no idea that you are eating cheesy eggs while you are eating.

Do chaffles just taste like burnt eggs and cheese?

The scent of cooking eggs is intolerable to me. My husband isn't permitted to prepare eggs in our home because he always allows the bottoms to become brown and burnt, and the smell makes me sick.

Egg and mozzarella cheese chaffles have a waffle-like flavor. The way to make them taste like a waffle is to add butter and sugar-free syrup to the batter. They've been a big hit with my family. The other day, my kid insisted on having them for breakfast.

What other types of chaffles can you make?

You have no idea what you could do with these resources, my friends.

Make a cheddar flavored savory chaffle with an egg and cheddar cheese that may be used as a hamburger bun, in a BLT, or as a substitute for bread in sandwiches.

Brownie chaffles may be made by mixing in chocolate powder. If you want the recipe as soon as it's available, sign up for my newsletter.

Make pumpkin chaffles by mixing them with pumpkin puree. If you want the recipe as soon as it's available, sign up for my newsletter.

Chaffles are made with garlic bread. Chaffles with pizza as the filling. Cookie chafes a lot of fun.

Make a chaffle for every occasion and go crazy with it.

How do you make a chaffle?

Chaffles may be made with only two ingredients: one big egg and half a cup of mozzarella.

For my tastes, finely shredded cheese is preferable to thicker pieces; nevertheless, this may not be an issue for you.

In a bit of waffle maker, lay half of the batter and cook for 2-3 minutes while whisking the egg and adding the cheese. Proceed with the second batch of batter as before.

As they cool, they crisp up a little like a waffle. After taking them from the waffle maker, let them a minute or two to cool down.

If you want it to have a more bread-like texture, you may add more coconut flour or almond flour. Start with 1 teaspoon of each and then fine-tune it based on your tastes.

KETO CHAFFLE RECIPES

1. CLASSIC CHAFFLE RECIPE

PREP TIME: 2 minutes

COOK TIME: 3 minutes

SERVINGS: 2 Chaffles

Ingredients

- 1 egg
- ½ cup of shredded mozzarella cheese
- 2 tbsp almond flour
- ¼ tsp baking powder

Directions

1. Waffle maker, preheat.
2. Mix the almond flour, baking powder, and egg in a small bowl.
3. To blend, give everything a good stir.

4. Use a small waffle iron for cooking half of the batter. Take a lid on the pot and heat for 3 minutes or until the eggs are set. Repeat with the remaining batter and remove from the waffle maker.

Nutrition:

Calories per Serving

Total Fat 21.6 g

Saturated Fat 11.0 g

Trans Fat   0.0 g

Cholesterol   137.8 mg

Total Carbohydrates 3.2 g

Dietary Fiber 0.7 g

Total Sugars   1.0 g

Sodium   537.3 mg

Protein   18.3 g

2. ALMOND FLOUR CHAFFLE

Prep Time:5 minutes

Cook Time:10 minutes

Total Time:15 minutes

Servings: 6 Belgian waffles

Calories: 314

Ingredients

- 6 eggs
- 1 cup of 2% or 4% milkfat cottage cheese
- 4 ounces cream cheese softened
- 1 cup of almond flour
- ½ cup of coconut flour
- ⅓ cup of Joy Filled Eats Sweetener
- 2 tsp vanilla
- 1 tsp baking powder US Customary – Metric

Instructions

1. Prepare a waffle iron by preheating.
2. Mix all of the items until they are smooth and creamy in a blender. Purée until smooth, scraping down the sides as necessary. Blend until smooth.
3. Grease the waffle iron by spraying it with non - stick cooking spray. Place the waffle iron in the middle of the room (less if you are not using a Belgian waffle iron).
4. Cook till golden brown all the way through. The ready light on your waffle iron may already be on when this happens. Don't worry about it. Remove the waffle by loosening it gently with your hands.
5. Proceed with the second batch of batter as before.

Nutrition

Serving: 1large waffle | Calories: 314 | Carbohydrates: 12g | Protein: 15g | Fat: 22g | Saturated Fat: 7g | Cholesterol: 190mg | Sodium: 272mg | Potassium: 207mg | Fiber: 5g | Sugar: 3g | Calcium: 148mg | Iron: 1.9mg

3. CREAM CHEESE COCONUT FLOUR CHAFFLE

Prep Time:5 mins

Cook Time:5 mins

Servings: 4

Calories: 257kcal

Ingredients

- 4 ounces cream cheese softened
- 4 large eggs
- 4 tbsp coconut flour
- 1 tsp baking powder
- 1 tbsp melted butter
- 2 tsp vanilla
- 1 tbsp keto sugar
- 1 tbsp sugar-free cocoa

Instructions

1. Prepare the waffle iron by following the manufacturer's directions.
2. Use a whisk or a personal blender to thoroughly mix the eggs, cream cheese, and melted butter.
3. Mix all of the other ingredients in the bowl with the mixture and stir thoroughly.

4. If using a full-size iron, pour half of the batter into the hot waffle maker. If you're using a tiny waffle maker, cut back on the batter.

5. Sweet waffles can be made with the leftover batter and a few extra ingredients. This step is optional if you want to create savory waffles instead.

Nutrition

Servings: 4

Amount per Serving

Calories 257

Total fat 19.8

Saturated fat 11.6g

Cholesterol 225mg

Sodium 206mg

Total Carbohydrate 9.7g

Protein 10.5 g

4. CHEDDAR & HERB CHAFFLE

Prep Time 1 min

Cook Time 4 mins

Total Time 5 mins

Servings 2

Ingredients

- 2 eggs
- 113g (1 cup) mature cheddar cheese grated
- 2 tbsp almond flour
- 1 tsp Italian Herb Seasoning
- 1/4 tsp baking powder
- 1/4 tsp salt

Instructions

1. Spray a waffle iron lightly with cooking spray before preheating it.
2. Baking powder and salt are added to the egg mixture and whisked until thoroughly blended.
3. The waffle maker has to be cooked for 3-4 minutes until the butter is lightly browned and the waffles are cooked through.
4. Remove the waffle from the pan with care, and then make another one with the rest of the batter.

5. Allow for two minutes of cooling before using (to get crispier).
6. Serve & Enjoy!

Nutrition Facts:

Servings: 2

Calories: 339

Fat: 27.6g

Carbohydrates: 2.2g

Fiber: 0.8g

Net Carbs: 2.1g

Protein: 21.4g

5. GARLIC BREAD CHAFFLE

Yield 2 servings

Prep time 5 minutes

Cook time 10 minutes

Total time 15 minutes

Ingredients

- 1 large egg
- 1/2 cup of finely shredded mozzarella
- 1 tsp coconut flour
- ¼ tsp baking powder
- ½ tsp garlic powder

- 1 tbsp butter, melted
- 1/4 tsp garlic salt
- 2 tbsp Parmesan
- 1 tsp minced parsley

Instructions

1. Preheating your small waffle iron is as simple as plugging it in. Turn the oven on to 375 Fahrenheit.
2. In a mixing bowl, mix the egg, coconut flour, mozzarella, garlic powder, and baking powder
3. Cook for 3 minutes or until steam stops coming out of the waffle iron after adding half of the chaffle batter. A baking sheet is an excellent place to put the chaffle.
4. To make more chaffles, simply repeat the process with the leftover batter.
5. Brush the chaffles with a mixture of melted butter and garlic salt.
6. Add the Parmesan to the chaffles and serve.
7. To melt the cheese, bake the dish for 5 minutes in the oven.
8. Before serving, garnish with fresh parsley.

Nutrition Information:

YIELD: 2 servings SERVING SIZE: 1

Amount Per Serving: Calories: 186 Total Fat: 14g Saturated Fat: 8g Trans Fat: 0g Unsaturated Fat: 5g Cholesterol: 127mg Sodium: 590mg Carbohydrates: 3g Net Carbohydrates: 2g Fiber: 1g Sugar: 1g Sugar Alcohols: 0g Protein: 10g

6. GRILLED CHEESE CHAFFLE

Prep Time: 3 minutes

Cook Time: 10 minutes

Servings: 1 Chaffle Sandwich

Calories: 549kcal

Ingredients

- 1 egg
- 1/4 tsp garlic powder
- 1/2 cup of shredded cheddar
- 2 Slices American cheese or 1/4 cup shredded cheese
- 1 tbsp butter

Instructions

1. Set your Dash Mini Waffle Maker to the "heat" position.
2. Mix the beaten egg, garlic powder, and shredded cheddar cheese in a small bowl until well-combined.

3. Stir in half of the chaffle ingredients to the hot dash waffle maker after being cooked through. Take after 4 minutes of cooking.

4. Cook the dash tiny waffle maker for 4 minutes with the remaining chaffle ingredients added to the batter.
5. Once the chaffles are cooked, place a medium-sized pan on the stovetop.
6. Melt one spoonful of butter into the mixture and then add the rest of the ingredients. Place 1 chaffle in the pan once the butter has melted. Place the second chaffle on top of the first and top it with your favorite cheese.
7. To finish melting the cheese, heat the chaffle for 1 minute on one side, flip it over and cook for an additional one-two minutes on the other.
8. Taking the cheese from the skillet once it's melted is the only way to eat it.

Nutrition

Calories: 549kcal | Carbohydrates: 3g | Protein: 27g | Fat: 48g | Saturated Fat: 28g | Cholesterol: 295mg | Sodium: 1216mg | Potassium: 172mg | Sugar: 1g | Vitamin A: 1550IU | Calcium: 871mg | Iron: 1mg

7. PARMESAN GARLIC KETO CHAFFLES

Prep time: 5 minutes

Cook time: 4 minutes

Total time: 9 minutes

Ingredients

- 1 tbsp fresh garlic minced
- 2 tbsp butter
- 1-ounce cubed cream cheese,
- 2 tbsp almond flour
- 1 tsp baking soda
- 2 large eggs
- 1 tsp dried chives
- ½ cup of Parmesan shredded cheese,
- ¾ shredded mozzarella cheese,

Instructions

1. Melt butter and the cream cheese in a small skillet over low-medium heat. (divorce is permitted)
2. Place the garlic and cook, stirring regularly for approximately 2 minutes, until it begins to smell good. (wait for the separation to appear)
3. Waffle maker, preheat.
4. Set aside a small mixing bowl and mix the flour and baking soda
5. .
6. For an additional 60 seconds, add the butter mixture to the eggs and beat on high for 90 seconds.

7. Stir together flour mixture, dried chives, and cheeses in a large basin until thoroughly blended. Place to a serving platter and serve immediately.
8. Generously grease waffle maker with low-carb cooking spray.
9. Scoop ¼ cup of batter into the waffle maker closed and cook for about 4 minutes or until golden brown.
10. Add desired toppings and serve.

Nutrition Information

Yield:2

Serving Size:1

Amount Per Serving

Calories: 385

Total Fat: 33g

Saturated Fat:17g

Trans Fat:0g

Unsaturated Fat: 13g

Cholesterol: 254mg

Sodium: 1243mg

Carbohydrates: 5g

Fiber: 1g

Sugar: 1g

Protein: 19

8. HOT HAM & CHEESE CHAFFLES

Yield 2 waffles

Prep time: 5 minutes

Cook time: 6 minutes

Total time: 11 minutes

Ingredients

- 1 large egg
- 1/2 cup of shredded swiss cheese
- 1/4 cup of chopped deli ham
- ¼ tsp garlic salt
- 1 tbsp mayonnaise
- 2 tsp dijon mustard

Instructions

1. Preheat your waffle iron by connecting it to the wall outlet.
2. The egg should be beaten until it's smooth in a small bowl. Cheese, ham, and garlic salt all go in together in a large bowl.
3. Waffle irons can steam for 3-4 minutes or until the batter is set and the waffle is cooked through, depending on how hot they are.
4. Repeat with the remaining batter after removing the waffle to a dish.
5. To make a dipping sauce, mix the mayo and mustard.

6. The waffles can be sliced in half or quarters and served with the dip.

Nutrition Information:

YIELD: 1 SERVING SIZE: 1

Amount Per Serving: Calories: 435 Total Fat: 32g Saturated Fat: 13g Trans Fat: 0g Unsaturated Fat: 17g Cholesterol: 265mg Sodium: 1235mg Carbohydrates: 4g Net Carbohydrates: 4g Fiber: 0g Sugar: 1g Sugar Alcohols: 0g Protein: 31g

9. WHITE BREAD KETO CHAFFLE

Yield: 2 chaffles

Prep time: 2 minutes

Cook time: 8 minutes

Total time: 10 minutes

Ingredients

- 1 Egg
- 3 tbsp Almond Flour
- 1 tbsp Mayonnaise
- 1/4 tsp Baking Powder
- 1 tsp Water

Instructions

1. Make small waffles by preheating the waffle machine.
2. Whisk the egg until it is well-beaten in a small bowl.
3. Baking powder and water are in the almond flour mixture.

4. When the waffle maker is hot, gently pour in half of the batter and close the lid. Cook for 3-5 minutes, stirring occasionally.

5. With care, take the waffles from the machine and let them cool for about two minutes before serving.

6. For the second chaffle, follow the directions just as you did for the first.

Nutrition Information:

Yield: 2 Chaffles serving size: 1

Amount Per Serving:

Calories: 125 Total fat: 11.5g

Carbohydrates: 2g NET

Carbohydrates: 1g

Fiber: 1g

Protein: 5g

10. WONDER BREAD CHAFFLES

Prep Time: 3 mins Cook Time: 2 mins Total Time: 5 mins
Servings: 2 Chaffles Calories: 139kcal

Ingredients

- 1 egg
- 3 tbsp almond flour
- 1 tbsp mayo
- 1/4 tsp baking powder
- 2 tsp water

Instructions

1. Prepare the waffle machine by setting it to high heat.
2. Add almond flour, mayo, baking powder, and water to well-beaten eggs.
3. Nonstick cooking the spray should be sprayed on the waffle iron. Then, pour half the batter into the waffle maker, and wait for the machine to make a clicking noise to let you know it's finished. Then, with the second waffle, repeat the procedure.

Nutrition

Calories: 139kcal | Carbohydrates: 3g | Protein: 5g | Fat: 13g | Saturated Fat: 2g | Polyunsaturated Fat: 4g | Monounsaturated Fat: 2g | Trans Fat: 1g | Cholesterol: 85mg | Sodium: 129mg | Potassium: 32mg | Fiber: 1g | Sugar: 1g | Calcium: 64mg | Iron: 1mg

11. DAIRY FREE KETO CHAFFLE

Prep Time 2 minutes

Cook Time 3 minutes

Servings 3 mini chaffles

Calories 109kcal

Ingredients

- 1 tbsp coconut flour
- 1 tbsp beef gelatin powder
- pinch sea salt
- 2 large eggs
- 1 tbsp mayonnaise

Instructions

1. Coconut flour, beef gelatin, and salt should be mixed in a small bowl.
2. Add the eggs and mayo to the dry ingredients and mix well. Use avocado oil spray to coat the waffle machine.
3. Thirdly divide the batter and place one-third of it in the waffle maker. Wait 2 minutes after closing the lid for the light to go off. Make sure it's browned to your liking by checking it frequently. Spray the waffle maker with oil spray one more and take lightly to a plate. Make two more batter sections by repeating the process with the remaining two portions of batter.
4. To Serve instantly or store in the refrigerator later use as a sandwich.

Nutrition

Serving: 1chaffle | Calories: 109kcal | Carbohydrates: 2g | Protein: 7g | Fat: 8g | Saturated Fat: 2g | Cholesterol: 146mg | Sodium: 202mg | Potassium: 52mg | Fiber: 1g | Sugar: 1g | Vitamin A: 204IU | Calcium: 21mg | Iron: 1mg

12. SAVORY CHAFFLE

Prep Time 5 minutes

Cook Time 5 minutes

Servings 2 waffles

ingredients

- 1/2 cup of shredded cheese
- 2 eggs
- 1 tbsp almond flour
- 1/8 tsp baking powder
- Optional add-ins
- cooked chopped bacon
- green onions

Instructions

1. The waffle maker should be preheated before use.
2. Beat the eggs with a fork in a small bowl. Add the grated cheese, almond flour, and a dash of baking powder to the mixture and combine well. Mix until all ingredients are well-combined.
3. Just about half a cup of the batter should be added to the waffle maker. Allow the enchantment to take place by closing the lid.

4. When the light on your waffle maker turns green, or if you don't have one when you notice a lot of steam rising, turn the waffle maker on. Cooking the waffle till it's golden takes around 4 minutes.

The waffle maker that i used did not have a nonstick finish, so i used nonstick frying spray before pouring the ingredients into the waffle maker.

13. DAIRY FREE AND EGG FREE CHAFFLE BREAD

Prep time:1 min

Cook time:3 mins

Servings:1 slice

INGREDIENTS

- 3 tbsp almond flour
- 1 tbsp veganaise
- 1/8 tsp baking powder
- 1/4 cup of just egg an egg replacer

INSTRUCTIONS

1. In a small bowl, add all the items and stir well until well-combined.
2. Add half of the ingredients to the tiny Dash waffle maker and preheat it.
3. Cooking time should be no more than three minutes.
4. Place on a cooling rack and allow to cool completely before handling.
5. Make a second loaf of bread using the remaining batter.

14. TRADITIONAL KETO LOW CARB CHAFFLE

Prep Time 5 mins

Cook Time 8 mins

Servings: 1

Calories: 291kcal

Ingredients

- 1 egg
- 1/2 cup of shredded cheddar cheese,

Instructions

1. Wipe off and lubricate all sides of the waffle maker before using.
2. Put the ingredients in a small bowl and mix well with 1/2 cup of the cheddar cheese.
3. Instead of using the entire egg, use just the white for a crispier chaffle.
4. Close the top of the waffle maker after adding half of the batter.
5. For best results, cook for 3-4 minutes, depending on the desired doneness of the dish.

6. Take carefully from the waffle maker and allow to cool for 2-3 minutes before serving.

7. Make a second chaffle by following the directions once more.

8. This classic chaffle recipe yields delicious sandwiches when used as directed.

Nutrition

Serving: 1g | Calories: 291kcal | Carbohydrates: 1g | Protein: 20g | Fat: 23g | Saturated Fat: 13g | Cholesterol: 223mg | Sodium: 413mg | Potassium: 116 mg | Sugar: 1g | Calcium: 432mg | Iron: 1mg

15. KETO CHAFFLE BREAKFAST SANDWICH

Yield: 1

Prep time: 3 MINUTES

Cook time: 10 MINUTES

Total time: 13 MINUTE

INGREDIENTS
For the chaffles

- egg
- 1/2 cup of shredded Cheddar cheese,

For the sandwich

- 2 strips bacon
- 1 egg
- 1 slice Cheddar or American cheese.

INSTRUCTIONS

1. The waffle maker should be preheated as directed by the manufacturer.
2. Egg and shredded cheese should be mixed in a small mixing bowl. Stir everything together until it's well-combined.
3. Fill the waffle machine halfway with the waffle batter. Cook for three-four minutes, or until golden brown on the outside. Then use the remaining batter to complete the recipe.
4. To Cook the bacon until crisp in a large skillet over medium heat, flipping it over as necessary. Remove to a paper towel-lined sink to drain.
5. Fry the egg over medium heat in the saved bacon drippings in the same skillet. Cook for a predetermined amount of time, depending on the desired level of doneness.

6. Put the sandwich together and eat it!

Nutrition Information: YIELD: 1 SERVING SIZE: 1

Amount Per Serving: CALORIES: 658TOTAL FAT: 51gsaturated FAT: 25gtrans FAT: 1gunsaturated FAT:

21gcholesterol: 495mgsodium: 1356mgcarbohydrates: 6gfiber: 0gsugar: 2gprotein: 43g

16. SIMPLE KETO CHAFFLES

Prep Time 1 min

Cook Time 6 mins

Total Time 7 mins

Servings: 2

Calories: 174 kcal

Instructions

1. Set your tiny waffle maker to the "on" position.
2. Make an omelet by whisking together one egg, salt, and cheese in a bowl.
3. Pour half of the batter into the waffle machine after it's heated up.
4. Cook the chaffle for a couple of minutes on each side.
5. Make a second chaffle with the remaining batter by cooking the remaining half of it.
6. To firm up your chaffle, place it on a wire rack and let it there for 2 - 3 minutes.

Nutrition

Serves 2

Calories Per Serving: 169

Total Fat 13.4g

11%Sodium 251mg

0%Total Carbohydrate 1.2g

0%Dietary Fiber 0g

Sugars 0.3g

21%Protein 10.7g

17. BUFFALO CHICKEN CHAFFLE

Prep time 15 minutes

Cook time 4 minutes

Total time 19 minutes

INGREDIENTS

- ¼ cup of almond flour
- 1 tsp baking powder
- 2 large eggs
- ½ cup of shredded chicken
- ¼ cup of shredded mozzarella cheese,
- ¼ cup of Frank's Red Hot Sauce + optional 1 tbsp for topping
- ¾ cup of shredded sharp cheddar cheese,
- ¼ cup of crumbled feta cheese
- ¼ cup of diced celery,

INSTRUCTIONS

1. Set aside a small mixing bowl with the almond flour and baking powder.
2. Low carb nonstick spray the waffle machine once it has been preheated to medium/high heat.
3. put eggs to a large bowl and whisk until foamy.
4. To begin, combine spicy sauce and mayonnaise in a large mixing bowl.
5. Re-add the flour mixture after you've mixed it with the eggs until it's well-mixed
6. Finally, blend the shredded cheeses with the remaining ingredients until smooth.
7. Add the chicken shreds and mix everything until well-combined.
8. Cook chaffles until they are golden brown on the outside in a preheated waffle maker. It took around four minutes.
9. Repeat Step 7 until all the batter has been used up, then take from the waffle machine.
10. serve with celery and/or spicy sauce on top of the chaffles

Nutrition information: yield: 2 serving size: 1

Amount Per Serving: calories: 675 total fat: 52g saturated fat: 24g trans fat: 1g unsaturated fat: 22g cholesterol: 330mg sodium: 1917mg carbohydrates: 8g fiber: 2g sugar: 3g protein: 44g

18. CHEDDAR CHIVE CHAFFLES

Prep Time 5 minutes

Cook Time 3 minutes

Total Time 8 minutes

Servings 2

Calories 277 kcal

Ingredients

- 1 large egg
- ½ cup of cheddar cheese finely shredded
- ¼ cup of superfine almond flour
- 1 tsp chives finely chopped
- 1 pinch sea salt optional
- coconut oil nonstick spray

Instructions

1. Prepare the waffle machine by setting it to high heat.
2. Lightly whisk the egg in a small mixing basin.
3. Chives, almond flour, and cheddar cheese are all good additions to the batter now. Combine all ingredients in a mixing bowl and stir until well blended. Add the salt and mix well after each element has been added (if using)

4. Coconut oil may be sprayed on a waffle iron. Cook the chaffle for 3 to 4 minutes, or until golden brown and cooked through, on the waffle iron. When the steam from the waffle iron starts to slow down, it's time to start checking.

5. Cool the chaffle on a cooling rack after taking it from the waffle iron. Before serving, let the chaffle thoroughly cool.

Nutrition Facts

Cheddar Chive Keto Chaffles Recipe

Amount Per Serving (2 waffles)

Calories 277

Fat 22g

Saturated Fat 9g

Trans Fat 0g

Polyunsaturated Fat 1g

Monounsaturated Fat 6g

Cholesterol 231mg

Sodium 341mg

Potassium 109mg

Carbohydrates 3g

Fiber 1g

Sugar 0g

Protein 18g

19. LEMON RICOTTA POPPYSEED CHAFFLES

yield: 2 CHAFFLES

prep time: 2 MINUTES

cook time: 6 MINUTES

total time: 8 MINUTES

Ingredients

- For the chaffle:
- 1 large egg
- 2 tbsp finely ground almond flour
- 1/4 cup of part-skim ricotta cheese
- 1 tsp sugar (or sweetener of choice)
- 1/8 tsp poppy seeds
- 1/4 tsp fresh lemon zest

Instructions

1. THE WAFFLE IRON SHOULD BE PREHEATED.
2. When all of the ingredients are blended, pour them into a small bowl and whisk until smooth.
3. Place half of the mixture in the waffle well that has been warmed.
4. Cook for a further 2-3 minutes, or until the steam has subsided.
5. Continue with the rest of the batter.
6. If desired, top with more ricotta and fresh berries before serving.

20. CHOCOLATE CHIP VANILLA CHAFFLES

Prep Time 1 minute

Cook Time 4 minutes

Total Time 5 minutes

Servings: 1

INGREDIENTS

- ½ cup of pre-shredded/grated mozzarella
- 1 egg - medium
- 1 tbsp you can use as much granulated sweetness as you like or not at all
- 1 tsp vanilla extract
- 2 tbsp almond meal/flour
- 1 tbsp sugar-free chocolate chips

INSTRUCTIONS

1. Prepare the items in a mixing dish and combine them well.
2. Set the tiny waffle machine to "warm" before using it. Using a spray bottle, with the coat waffle maker, olive oil and pour in about half of the butter. Continue cooking for an additional 2-4 minutes before removing from heat and repeating with the remaining ingredients. Per recipe, you should be able to get 2 little pancakes out of it.
3. After that, all you have to do is serve and enjoy.

Nutrition Facts:
Amount per Serving

NET carbs 3.9g

Total Carbohydrates 5.4g

Fiber 1.5g

Sugar 1.8g

Protein 22.2g

Fat 20.1g

Sodium 412.6mg

Potassium 114.4m

21. SWEET CHOCOLATE CHAFFLE

Prep time 10 minutes

Cook time 25 minutes

Total time 35 minutes

Ingredients

- 1/4 cup of Cream Cheese
- Tbsp Almond Flour
- 1 tsp Baking Powder
- 1 Egg
- 1/2 tsp Vanilla Extract
- 1 Tbsp Sugar Substitute
- 1-2 Tbsp Cocoa

Instructions

1. Before you begin assembling, make sure all of your materials are ready to go. This will help the process go more easily.

2. The Dash tiny waffle maker may be heated at the same time as the food in the pan.
3. Whisk the egg and sweetener together until frothy using an electric hand mixer.
4. Once the egg and sweetener are mixed, add the other ingredients.
5. To get a frothy, smooth texture, mix all ingredients in a mixing bowl and whisk until well mixed.
6. Apply a little layer of oil to your Dash tiny waffle maker.
7. The mixture should be between 1 and 1 1/2 tbsp.
8. Mix the ingredients evenly with the back of a spoon and the whole Chaffle maker.
9. Cook for 4 to 5 minutes until the light goes out, or you can open the Chaffle maker freely without it sticking. Gently close the lid.

Nutrition Information

Yield:5

Serving Size:1

Amount Per Serving

Calories 81

Total Fat 7g

Carbohydrates 2g

Protein 3g

22. RASPBERRY ALMOND CHAFFLES

Prep time: 10 mins

Cook time: 6 mins

Servings: 1

Calories 395 kcal

INGREDIENTS

- 1 large egg
- 1-ounce cream cheese
- 2 tbsp almond flour
- 1/3 cup of raspberries divided
- 1 tbsp Confectioner's Swerve
- 1/4 tsp baking powder
- 1/2 tsp almond extract divided
- 1 small pinch of salt
- 2 tbsp heavy cream
- 1 tsp Sukrin Gold Fiber Syrup or another sweetener of choice

INSTRUCTIONS

1. Get your mini-waffle iron (Dash) ready by preheating it.
2. Fill your blender halfway with all of the ingredients and mix until smooth. Then add the remaining 1/4 teaspoon almond extract and baking powder. Preheat the Dash and pour half the batter in. Cook for about 3 minutes, or until the light shuts off. Repeat with the remaining batter after gently removing the pancakes with a fork onto a platter.
3. While the second waffle is baking, mix the heavy cream, 1/4 cup almond flour, and Sukrin Gold or another sweetener of your choice. To produce soft peaks, whisk

the cream until it forms a ribbon held in your hand or with an electric mixer. Then, when the second waffle is done, add the remaining cream and raspberries to both waffles and serve right away.

Macros per Serving (2 chaffles): 395 calories, 4 grams net carbs, 11 grams protein, 35 grams fat.

23. CHOCOLATE CUPCAKE CHAFFLE

Servings:2

Prep time: 3minutes

Cooking time: 3minutes

Calories: 82kcal

INGREDIENTS

- 1 large egg, beaten
- 2 TB dark cocoa powder
- 2 TB granulated sweetener (I prefer BochaSweet)
- 1/4 tsp baking powder
- 1/2 tsp vanilla extract
- 1 TB heavy whipping cream

DIRECTIONS

1. Whip together all of the items until smooth and fluffy together in a bowl.
2. Cook for 3 minutes or until no more steam rises from the waffle maker after adding half of the batter to the tiny waffle maker.
3. Allow cooling for 5-10 minutes on a cooling rack.
4. For a second chaffle, follow steps 2 and 3 again.

5. To create an excellent dessert sandwich, you may combine two tbsp of softened cream cheese with a similar amount of sweetened Swerve confectioner's sugar and add 1/4 tsp vanilla extract to it. For two "sandwiches," you'll have plenty of icing.

24. CHOCOLATE CHIP CHAFFLES

Prep Time: 3 minutesCook Time: 8 minutes Servings: 2 keto chaffles

Ingredients

- 1/2 cup of shredded mozzarella cheese
- 1 tbsp almond flour
- 1 egg
- 1/4 tsp cinnamon
- 1/2 tbsp Granulated Swerve
- 2 tbsp low carb chocolate chips like Lily's chocolate chips

Instructions

1. Connect your waffle maker to the power source.
2. Make an egg white omelet by whisking the almond flour, milk, and vanilla extract in a small bowl.
3. Dish Mini waffle maker: use half the keto chocolate chip Chaffle batter at a time. For 4 minutes, cook the chaffle batter in the waffle machine.
4. Cook the second one when the first is finished cooking.
5. To firm them up, place them on a platter and let them sit for 1-2 minutes. Simply eat it without any additional toppings, or add whipped cream or powdered sugar for a special touch.

Nutrition

Serving: 1g | Calories: 136kcal | Carbohydrates: 2g | Protein: 10g | Fat: 10g | Saturated Fat: 5g | Cholesterol: 104mg | Sodium: 207mg | Potassium: 52mg | Fiber: 1g | Sugar: 1g | Vitamin A: 308IU | Calcium: 161mg | Iron: 1mg

25. MAPLE PECAN KETO CHAFFLES

Prep Time 5 minutes

Cook Time 5 minutes

Total Time 10 minutes

Servings 2

Ingredients

- 1 large egg
- 1/2 cup of shredded mozzarella cheese finely
- 1/4 cup almond flour
- 1 tbsp pecans
- 1 tbsp brown allulose/monk fruit
- 2-3 drops maple flavoring
- coconut oil, no-stick spray
-

Instructions

1. Warm-up a mini-waffle maker.
2. In a small mixing dish, softly whisk the egg. Combine mozzarella cheese, almond flour, nuts, sweetener, and maple flavoring in a mixing bowl. Mix until the batter is well mixed.

3. Coconut oil should be sprayed on the waffle iron. Close the waffle iron after scooping half of the batter onto it— Cook for 3 to 4 minutes, or until the chaffle is golden brown and well cooked. When the steam from the waffle iron begins to slow, it's a good time to start checking.

4. Put the chaffle on a cooling rack after taking it from the waffle iron. Before serving, let the chaffle cool fully.

Nutrition Facts
Amount Per Serving (1 waffle)

Calories 162 Calories

Fat 12g

Saturated Fat 4g

Trans Fat 0g

Polyunsaturated Fat 1g

Monounsaturated Fat 2g

Cholesterol 108mg

Sodium 206mg

Potassium 50mg

Carbohydrates 2g

Fiber 1g

Sugar 0g

Protein 12

26. YOGURT CHAFFLES

Prep time 5 mins

Cook time 4 mins

Total time 9 mins

Servings 1 chaffle

INGREDIENTS

- 1 egg
- ½ cup of + 2 tbsp shredded cheese divided
- 2 tbsp almond flour
- ¼ tsp baking powder
- 1 tbsp plain whole fat yogurt

INSTRUCTIONS

1. Mix the egg, baking powder, almond flour, and yogurt in a large mixing basin. To mix, whisk until well combined.
2. Preheat a tiny or standard waffle iron and oil if necessary. Fill the waffle iron halfway with grated cheese. Add 13 of the batter (approximately two heaping teaspoons) and, if preferred, another sprinkling of cheese.
3. Cook the chaffles for 3-4 minutes under a lid, or until they are crisp and brown.
4. Serve alone or with toppings like avocados, tomatoes, yogurt, and scallions.

NUTRITION

Calories: 323kcal, Carbohydrates: 6g, Protein: 22g, Fat: 24g, Saturated Fat: 10g, Trans Fat: 1g, Cholesterol: 211mg, Sodium:

424mg, Potassium: 235mg, Fiber: 2g, Sugar: 2g, Vitamin A: 636IU, Vitamin C: 1mg, Calcium: 404mg, Iron: 2mg

27. KETO GINGERBREAD CHAFFLE

Prep time:5 mins

Cook time: 5 mins

Servings:2

Calories: 207 kcal

INGREDIENTS

- ½ cup of mozzarella cheese grated
- 1 medium egg
- ½ tsp baking powder
- 1 tsp erythritol powdered
- ½ tsp ginger, ground
- ¼ tsp nutmeg, ground
- ½ tsp cinnamon, ground
- ⅛ tsp ground cloves,
- 2 tbsp almond flour

INSTRUCTIONS

1. Lightly lubricate your waffle machine and turn it on (I give it a light spray with olive oil)
2. In a mixing bowl, whisk the egg.
3. Mix the mozzarella, almond flour, spices, baking powder, and erythritol in a mixing bowl. Mix thoroughly.

4. The batter should be poured into your waffle machine and spread out evenly to achieve the best results. (If you have a smaller waffle machine, use half of the ingredients to create one waffle and then repeat.)
5. Close the cover and cook for five minutes.
6. Remove the cooked waffles with tongs.
7. Garnish with whipped cream or cream cheese icing if desired.

NUTRITION

Serving: 1waffleCalories: 207kcalCarbohydrates: 5.7gProtein: 12.2gFat: 15.9gFiber: 2.2g

---

28. BLUEBERRY CHAFFLES

Prep Time: 2 minutes

Cook Time: 5 minutes

Total Time: 7 minutes

INGREDIENTS

- 1 tbsp of almond flour
- 1 egg
- 1 tsp vanilla
- 1 shake of cinnamon
- 1 tsp baking powder
- 1 cup of mozzarella cheese (total fat, skim or nonfat will work depending on your preferences).
- 1/4 cup of blueberries

INSTRUCTIONS

1. In a mixing dish, combine the egg and vanilla essence.

2. Mix the baking powder, almond flour, and cinnamon in a mixing bowl.
3. Finally, coat the mozzarella cheese evenly with the mixture.
4. Fold in the blueberries with care.
5. Spray the waffle maker with oil and heat it to the highest setting.
6. Cook the waffle, inspecting it every 5 minutes until it becomes crispy and brown. Please remember to just use half of the butter. The waffle maker tends to overflow, making the operation untidy. I recommend laying down a Silpat mat for easy cleanup.
7. Remove it with care and top with butter and your favorite low-carb syrup.

Nutrition Information: YIELD: 2

Amount Per Serving: CALORIES: 380

29. PEANUT BUTTER CHAFFLE

yield: 2

prep time: 5 minutes

cook time: 5 minutes

total time: 10 minutes

Ingredients

- 1 egg
- 2 tbsp all-natural peanut butter

- 1 tbsp heavy cream
- 1/2 tsp almond extract
- 1 tsp coconut flour
- 1/4 tsp baking powder

Instructions

1. Mix all items and place them in a waffle maker that has been warmed. Cook for 4 minutes, or until no steam is escaping from the sides of the waffle machine.

2. Enjoy with sugar-free strawberry jam or your favorite topping!

Nutrition Information: YIELD: 2

Amount Per Serving: CALORIES: 380

30. KETO CHAFFLE GLAZED DONUT

Prep time 10 mins

Cook time 5 mins

Total time 15 mins

Servings 3

INGREDIENTS
For the chaffles

- ½ cup of Mozzarella cheese shredded
- 1-ounce Cream Cheese

- tbsp Unflavored whey protein isolate
- 2 tbsp Swerve confectioners sugar substitute
- ½ tsp Baking powder
- ½ tsp Vanilla extract
- 1 Egg

For the glaze topping:

- tbsp Heavy whipping cream
- 3-4 tsp Swerve confectioners sugar substitute
- ½ tsp Vanilla extract

INSTRUCTIONS

1. Warm-up your tiny waffle maker.
2. In a microwave-safe bowl, mix the mozzarella and cream cheese. Slowly bring to a boil for 30 seconds at a time, stirring constantly until the cheeses are melted and well mixed.
3. To the cheese mixture, add the whey protein, 2 tbsp Swerve confectioners sugar, and baking soda and knead till mixed using your hands.
4. In a mixing basin, combine the dough, egg, and vanilla extract until a homogeneous batter develops.
5. Place one-third of the batter in the micro waffle machine and cook for 3-5 minutes, or until done to your liking.
6. Step 5 should be repeated with the remaining 23 of the batter, for a total of 3 chaffles.

7. Mix the glaze topping ingredients and pour over the chaffles before serving.

31. CHOCOLATE CHIP CHAFFLES

Yield 2 chaffles

Prep time 5 minutes

Cook time 6 minutes

Total time 11 minutes

Ingredients

- 1 large egg
- 1 tsp coconut flour
- 1 tsp monk fruit sweetener
- 1/2 tsp vanilla extract
- 1/2 cup of finely shredded mozzarella
- tbsp sugar-free chocolate chips

Instructions

1. Preheat your waffle maker by plugging it in.
2. Pour all four ingredients into a small mixing bowl and use a fork to mix them.
3. Add the shredded cheese and mix well.
4. Put half of the butter in the waffle iron and half of the chocolate chips on top before you start cooking. Each chocolate chip should have a thin layer of butter on top of it.
5. Close the waffle oven and cook for 3-4 minutes, or until the waffles are as crisp as you desire.
6. Rep with the remaining batter.

7. Serve with whipped cream or low carb ice cream while it's still hot.

Nutrition Information: YIELD: 1 SERVING SIZE: 2 waffles

Amount Per Serving: Calories: 304Total Fat: 16gSaturated Fat: 8gTrans Fat: 0gUnsaturated Fat: 6gCholesterol: 216mgSodium: 375mgCarbohydrates: 7gNet Carbohydrates: 3gFiber: 0gSugar: 0gSugar Alcohols: 4gProtein: 17g

32. LEMON CAKE CHAFFLES

Prep Time: 2 minutes

Cook Time: 6 minutes

Total Time: 8 minutes

Servings: 2 waffles

Ingredients

- 1 tbsp Coconut Flour
- tsp Monkfruit
- 1/4 tsp Baking Powder
- 1 Egg room temp
- 1-ounce Cream Cheese room temp
- 1/2 tsp Lemon Extract
- 1/2 tsp Vanilla Extract

Instructions

1. Collect all of the components. Submerge the egg in warm water for three-five minutes for rapid room temperature

eggs. Take the quantity needed for fast room temperature cream cheese and microwave for 10-15 seconds.
2. Preheat the Dash Mini Waffle Maker.
3. Mix Coconut Flour, Monkfruit, and Baking Powder in a small mixing basin.
4. Next, whisk the egg, cream cheese, lemon extract, and vanilla extract until thoroughly blended.
5. Pour butter into waffle iron and cook for three-four minutes, or until the desired browning. Serve with your favorite sugar-free syrup or on its own!

Nutrition

Calories: 98kcal | Carbohydrates: 3g | Protein: 4g | Fat: 7g | Saturated Fat: 4g | Trans Fat: 1g | Cholesterol: 97mg | Sodium: 137mg | Potassium: 52mg | Fiber: 1g | Sugar: 1g | Vitamin A: 309IU | Calcium: 56mg | Iron: 1mg

33. KETO OREO CHAFFLES

Prep Time 10 mins

Cook Time 4 mins

Total Time 14 mins

Servings 4

Calories 237

Ingredients
For the chaffles:

- 1 cup of Mozzarella cheese shredded
- large eggs
- 2 tbsp Swerve confectioners sugar substitute

- 2 tbsp unsweetened cocoa powder, preferably black cocoa powder

- ***For the topping:***
  - ounces Cream cheese softened
  - tbsp Heavy whipping cream
  - tbsp Swerve confectioners sugar substitute

Instructions

1. Warm-up a tiny waffle maker.
2. In a small blender, purée the chaffle ingredients until smooth. To fully mix the ingredients, use a mixing bowl and a whisk.
3. 14 of the butter should be placed in the tiny waffle maker at a time and cooked for three-four minutes each until done.
4. To make the topping, mix all of the ingredients in a blender and blend until smooth.
5. Serve each chaffle with the topping, either separately or piled on top of each other and sliced into fourths.

Notes

The chaffle components are best mixed in a smoothie mixer.

Use two waffle machines at the same time to create the chaffles faster.

Make a big batch of these chaffles and store them in the freezer for later use to save time.

Cook the chaffles for a little longer or place them in the toaster for a minute or two after they're done.

It can be refrigerated for 5 - 7 days or frozen for up to six months.

34. KETO PUMPKIN CHAFFLES

Prep Time 2 mins

Cook Time 5 mins

Total Time 7 mins

Calories: 250

Servings:1

INGREDIENTS

- ½ cup of shredded mozzarella cheese
- beaten whole egg,
- ½ tbsp pumpkin purée
- ½ tsp Swerve confectioners
- ½ tsp vanilla extract
- ¼ tsp Pumpkin Pie Spice, see my recipe
- ⅛ tsp pure maple extract, see notes

INSTRUCTIONS

1. Start preparing the batter in your Waffle Maker (mine makes 4" waffles).
2. In a mixing basin, whisk together all of the ingredients except the mozzarella cheese. Mix in the cheese until thoroughly mixed.
3. Spray your waffle irons with nonstick cooking spray (I used coconut oil) and pour half of the batter into the

center. Close the top and cook the Chaffles for 4-6 minutes, depending on how crispy you like your Chaffles.

4. Remove the first Chaffle and cook the second. Serve with butter, Sugar-Free Maple Syrup, toasted nuts, a sprinkle of ground cinnamon, a dollop of whip cream, or any mix thereof.

Nutrition Facts

Keto Pumpkin Chaffles

Amount Per Serving

Calories 250 Calories from Fat 135

Fat 15g

Saturated Fat 8g

Carbohydrates 5g

Fiber 1g

Sugar 1g

Protein 23g

35. BLACKBERRIES AND CREAM CHAFFLE

prep time: 7 minutes

cook time: 15 minutes

total time: 22 minutes

Ingredients

- ounces cream cheese, softened
- 1 tbsp monk-fruit sweetener
- 1 tsp vanilla extract
- 1/4 cup of fresh blackberries, washed and dried
- large eggs
- tbsp coconut flour
- 1 tsp baking powder
- 1/2 cup of mozzarella shredded cheese

Instructions

1. Preheat your waffle maker to medium/high and spray it with low carb nonstick spray.
2. Microwave cream cheese in a small heat-proof basin for 25 seconds on 50% power. In a large mixing bowl, mix warmed cream cheese, blackberries, sugar, and vanilla, and beat with a hand mixer until creamy.
3. In a separate mixing dish, beat the eggs until foamy.
4. In a small mixing basin, combine the flour and baking powder.

5. Add the flour mixture and cream cheese mixture to the egg mixture and whisk for another minute.
6. Mix in the mozzarella until well mixed.
7. 14 cups of batter should be placed in a prepared waffle maker.
8. Cook for approximately 3-4 minutes, or until golden brown.
9. Continue with the remaining batter.

Nutrition Information

Yield 2

Serving Size 1 Amount Per Serving Calories412

Total Fat 31g Saturated Fat 17g Trans Fat 0g Unsaturated Fat 11g Cholesterol 257mg Sodium 647mg Carbohydrates 16g Fiber 2g Sugar 7g Protein 17g

36. KETO STRAWBERRY SHORTCAKE CHAFFLE

yield: 2 chaffles

prep time: 2 minutes

cook time: 4 minutes

total time: 6 minutes

Ingredients

- 1 Egg
- 1 tbsp Heavy Whipping Cream
- 1 tsp Coconut Flour
- tbsp Lakanto Golden Sweetener (Use butter together for 20% off)
- 1/2 tsp Cake Batter Extract
- 1/4 tsp Baking powder

Instructions

1. Warm up the tiny waffle maker.
2. Mix all chaffle ingredients in a small bowl.
3. Half of the chaffle batter should be poured into the center of the waffle iron. Allow for 3-5 minutes of cooking time. If the chaffle rises, lift the lid slightly for a few seconds until it begins to fall back down, then replace the cover until it finishes.
4. Remove with care and repeat for the second chaffle. Allow the chaffles to rest for a few minutes to crisp up.
5. Enjoy with as much whipped cream and strawberries as you like!

Nutrition Information:

YIELD: 2 Mini Chaffles serving size: 1

Amount Per Serving:

CALORIES: 59

TOTAL FAT: 4.6g

Carbohydrates: 0.75g NET

FIBER: 0.25g

PROTEIN: 3.2g

37. PUMPKIN CHOCOLATE CHIP CHAFFLES

Prep Time: 4 minutes

Cook Time: 12 minutes

Servings: 3 chaffles

Ingredients

- 1/2 cup of shredded mozzarella cheese
- tsp pumpkin puree
- 1 egg
- tbsp granulated Swerve
- 1/4 tsp pumpkin pie spice
- tsp sugar-free chocolate chips
- 1 tbsp almond flour

Instructions

1. Connect your waffle maker.
2. Mix the pumpkin puree and egg in a small mixing bowl. Make sure all of the pumpkins is mixed with the egg.
3. Mix in the mozzarella cheese, almond flour, swerve, and pumpkin spice.
4. Then stir in the sugar-free chocolate chips.
5. Half of the keto pumpkin pie At a time, place the chaffle mix to the bowl mini waffle maker. In a waffle machine, cook the chaffle batter for 4 minutes.
6. Do not open before the end of the four minutes. You mustn't open the waffle machine before 4 minutes. After that, you may open it to examine it and make sure it's fully cooked, but with these chaffles, keeping the lid closed the entire time is critical.

7. Cook the second one after the first one has finished cooking.

8. Swerve confectioners' sweetener or whipped cream over the top, if desired.

Nutrition

Serving: 1g | Calories: 93kcal | Carbohydrates: 2g | Protein: 7g | Fat: 7g | Saturated Fat: 3g | Cholesterol: 69mg | Sodium: 138mg | Potassium: 48mg | Fiber: 1g | Sugar: 1g | Vitamin A: 1228IU | Calcium: 107mg | Iron: 1mg

38. CHOCOLATE CHIP CHAFFLE

Prep Time 5 mins

Cook Time 8 mins

Servings: 1

Calories: 146kcal

Ingredients

- 1 egg
- 1 tbsp heavy whipping cream
- 1/2 tsp coconut flour
- 1 3/4 tsp Lakanto monk fruit golden can use more or less to adjust sweetness
- 1/4 tsp baking powder
- pinch of salt

- 1 tbsp Lily's Chocolate Chips

Instructions

1. Turn on the waffle machine to warm it up.
2. In a small mixing basin, blend all of the ingredients except the chocolate chips until thoroughly incorporated.
3. Grease the waffle machine, then pour half of the batter onto the waffle maker's bottom plate. Close the container with a few chocolate chips on top.
4. Cook for 3-4 minutes, or until the chocolate chip chaffle dessert is golden brown, then remove with a fork. keeping an eye out for charred skin on your fingertips.
5. Repeat with the remaining batter.
6. Allow the chaffle to rest for a few minutes to crisp up. Serve with sugar-free whipped topping if preferred.

Nutrition

Serving: 1g | Calories: 146kcal | Carbohydrates: 7g | Protein: 6g | Fat: 10g | Saturated Fat: 7g | Fiber: 3g | Sugar: 1g

39. BROWNIE CHOCOLATE CHAFFLE

Prep Time :1 min

Cook Time:9 mins

Total Time: 10 mins

Servings: 1

Calories: 188kcal

Ingredients

- 1 Egg Whisked
- 1/3 cup of Mozzarella Cheese Shredded
- ½ tbsp Cocoa Powder Dutch Processed (regular is okay too)
- 1 tbsp Almond Flour
- 1 tbsp Monkfruit Sweetener (add an extra tsp if you like your treats sweeter)
- 1/4 tsp Vanilla extract
- 1/4 tsp Baking Powder
- Pinch Salt

Instructions

1. Warm-up your tiny waffle iron.
2. Whisk the egg in a mixing basin. Mix in the dry ingredients. Then stir in the cheese.
3. (Optional) place 2 tsp heavy cream into the mixture if you want a moist brownie waffle.

4. 1/3 of the batter should be poured onto the waffle iron. Cook for three minutes, or until the steam from the waffle iron stops.

5. Allow cooling slightly on a wire rack.

6. Serve with your preferred low-carb toppings.

Nutrition

Serves 1

Calories Per Serving: 188

Total Fat 7.1g

22%Sodium 509.7mg

3%Total Carbohydrate 8.9g

14%Dietary Fiber 4g

Sugars 1.3g

42%Protein 20.8g

40. COFFEE CAKE CHAFFLES
Ingredients

- 1 TBSP Butter, salted, melted (CHAFFLE)
- ½ tsp Vanilla extract (CHAFFLE)
- ⅛ tsp Baking powder (CHAFFLE)
- TBSP And I Like It™ FirstRate™ (CHAFFLE)
- 1 Egg, large (CHAFFLE)

- 2 TBSP And I Like It™ Baking Blend, packed (CHAFFLE)
- 1 TBSP melted butter, salted (CRUMBLE)
- 1 tsp And I Like It™ FirstRate™ (CRUMBLE)
- ½ tsp Cinnamon, ground (CRUMBLE)
- 1 TBSP chopped Pecans (CRUMBLE)

Directions

1. Plug in your tiny waffle maker (a little griddle can also work) coat with nonstick cooking spray.
2. Butter, vanilla, baking powder, and FirstRate
3. are all mixed in a small mixing bowl.
4. Add the egg and Baking Blend, whisking until just mixed.
5. In a small mixing bowl, mix all of the crumble ingredients.
6. Pour half of the chaffle batter onto your tiny waffle maker, followed by half of the crumble.
7. Cook for 3-5 minutes, or until the steaming stops.
8. Rep for the second chaffle.

41. PUMPKIN PECAN CHAFFLE

PREP TIME 2 mins

COOK TIME 8 mins

TOTAL TIME 10 mins

SERVINGS 2 servings

CALORIES 210 kcal

INGREDIENTS

- 1 egg
- ½ cup of mozzarella cheese grated
- 1 tsp pumpkin puree
- ½ tsp pumpkin spice
- 1 tsp erythritol low carb sweetener
- tbsp almond flour
- 2 tbsp toasted chopped pecans,

INSTRUCTIONS

1. Turn on your waffle machine and lightly grease it (I lightly spray it with olive oil). In a separate dish, whip the egg.
2. Mix in the mozzarella, pumpkin, almond flour, pumpkin spice, and erythritol.
3. Add the pecan bits and mix well.
4. Spread the batter out evenly in your waffle maker.
5. (If you have a smaller waffle machine, use half of the ingredients to create one waffle and then repeat.)
6. Close the cover and cook for five minutes.
7. Remove the cooked waffles with tongs.
8. Serve with whipped cream or low-carb caramel sauce on the side. Maybe some pecan nuts.

42. KETO RED VELVET CHAFFLES

yield: 4 chaffles

prep time: 10 minutes

Cook time: 5 minutes

Total time: 15 minutes

Ingredients

For Chaffles

- 1 cup of Mozzarella Cheese, shredded
- Large Eggs
- 1/2 tsp Vanilla Extract
- 2 tbsp Lakanto Powdered Sweetener
- 2 tbsp Cocoa Powder, unsweetened
- Red food coloring, optional

For Icing

- ounces. Cream Cheese, softened
- 2 tbsp Lakanto Powdered Sweetener
- 1/2 tsp Vanilla Extract

Instructions

1. Warm-up your tiny waffle maker.
2. In a mixing basin, mix all of the chaffle ingredients and whisk thoroughly. Add enough food coloring to the batter to give it a rich crimson hue.
3. 14 of the batter should be placed in the hot waffle machine and cooked till done to your preference.
4. Step 3 should be repeated until all of the butter has been utilized.

5. To make the icing, put all ingredients in a mixing bowl and whisk until smooth and creamy.
6. Spread the frosting on top of each chaffle before serving.

Nutrition

yield: 4 chaffles

serving size: 1 chaffle

Amount per serving: calories: 197 total fat: 15.2g carbohydrates: 3.25gnet carbohydrates: 2.25g fiber: 1g Protein: 11.75g

43. PEANUT BUTTER CHOCOLATE CHIP CHAFFLE

Prep Time: 2 minutes

Cook Time: 8 minutes

Servings: 2 chaffles

Ingredients

- 1 egg.
- 1/4 cup of shredded mozzarella cheese
- tbsp creamy Peanut Butter.
- 1 tbsp Almond Flour.
- 1 tbsp Granulated Swerve.
- 1 tsp Vanilla extract.
- 1 tbsp low carb chocolate chips

Instructions

1. Connect your waffle maker.
2. Mix the peanut butter and egg in a small mixing bowl. Make sure all of the peanut butter is mixed with the egg.
3. Mix in the mozzarella cheese, almond flour, swerve, and chocolate chips.
4. Mix with half of the keto peanut butter chocolate chip. At a time, put chaffle mix to the Bowl Mini waffle maker. In a waffle machine, cook the chaffle batter for 4 minutes.
5. Cook the second one after the first one has finished cooking.
6. Swerve confectioners' sweetener or whipped cream over the top, if desired.

Nutrition

Serving: 1g | Calories: 193kcal | Carbohydrates: 5g | Protein: 11g | Fat: 15g | Saturated Fat: 4g | Cholesterol: 93mg | Sodium: 193mg | Potassium: 134mg | Fiber: 1g | Sugar: 2g | Vitamin A: 213IU | Calcium: 97mg | Iron: 1mg

44. KETO CINNAMON ROLL CHAFFLES

yield: 3 chaffles

prep time: 10 minutes

cook time: 5 minutes

total time: 15 minutes

Ingredients

For the chaffles:

- 1/3 cup of Mozzarella Cheese, shredded
- 2 ounces Cream Cheese
- 2 tbsp Lakanto Monkfruit Sweetener
- 1 tbsp Coconut Flour
- 1/4 tsp Baking Powder
- 1/4 tsp Cinnamon
- 1/2 tsp Vanilla Extract
- 1 Egg

For the icing

- 1 tbsp Heavy Whipping Cream
- 2-3 tbsp Lakanto Powdered Monkfruit Sweetener
- 1/2 tbsp Lakanto Monkfruit Sweetener, classic
- 1/4 tsp Cinnamon

Instructions

1. Warm-up your tiny waffle maker.
2. In a microwave-safe bowl, mix the mozzarella and cream cheeses. Stir the cheeses after every 30 seconds in the microwave until they are melted and well mixed.
3. Incorporate the coconut flour, baking powder, Swerve sweetener, cinnamon, and vanilla essence into the cheese mixture until thoroughly mixed.
4. In a mixing bowl, mix the dough and one egg, and beat on high until smooth.

5. 13 of the batter should be added to the hot tiny waffle maker and cooked for a few minutes or until the desired amount of doneness is obtained.
6. Step 5 should be repeated with the remaining batter until three chaffles are produced.
7. On high, mix the heavy whipping cream and confectioners sugar substitute until the required consistency is attained.
8. Drizzle the icing all over the chaffles.
9. Before serving, mix the granulated sugar and cinnamon and sprinkle on top of the chaffles

Nutrition Information:

YIELD: 3 SERVING SIZE: 1

Amount Per Serving: CALORIES: 195TOTAL FAT: 17.2gcarbohydrates: 4.7gnet CARBOHYDRATES: 3.67gfiber: 1.03gprotein: 7.3g

45. KETO BANANA NUT CHAFFLES

yield: 1

prep time: 10 minutes

cook time: 4 minutes

total time: 14 minutes

Ingredients

- 1 Tbsp Heavy Whipping Cream
- 1 Tbsp Lakanto Powdered Sweetener
- 1 Tbsp Coconut Flour
- 1 Egg, Large

- ½ tsp Vanilla Extract
- 1 tsp Banana Extract
- 1 Tbsp chopped Walnuts,
- Optional - 1 Tbsp ChocZero Sugar-Free Maple Syrup

Instructions

1. Warm-up your tiny waffle maker.
2. In a mixer bowl, mix all the chaffle ingredients except the walnuts and blend on high until smooth.
3. Pour the batter into the micro waffle machine and fold in the walnuts.
4. Cook for 2-4 minutes, or until the chaffle is done to your liking.
5. If preferred, top with a drizzle of sugar-free maple syrup and a few additional chopped walnuts.

Nutrition Information:

YIELD: 1 SERVING SIZE: 1

Amount Per Serving: CALORIES: 341TOTAL FAT: 31.8gCARBOHYDRATES: 5.5gNET CARBOHYDRATES: 3gFIBER: 2.5gPROTEIN: 9.5g

46. KETO CREAM CHEESE MINI CHAFFLE WAFFLES

Prep Time: 3 minutes

Cook Time: 8 minutes

Total Time: 11 minutes

Servings: 2 Waffle

Calories: 73kcal

Ingredients

- tsp Coconut Flour
- tsp Swerve/Monkfruit
- 1/4 tsp Baking Powder
- 1 Whole Egg room temp
- 1-ounce Cream Cheese room temp
- 1/2 tsp Vanilla Extract

Instructions

1. Collect all of the components. Submerge the egg in warm water for three- minutes for rapid room temperature eggs. Take the desired amount of room temperature cream cheese and microwave for 10-15 seconds.
2. Preheat the waffle iron.
3. Mix Coconut Flour, Swerve/Monkfruit, and baking powder in a small mixing basin.
4. Next, whisk together the egg, cream cheese, and vanilla extract until thoroughly blended.

5. Pour butter into waffle iron and cook for 3-4 minutes, or until the desired browning. Serve with your preferred waffle toppings.

Nutrition:

Calories: 73kcal

Carbohydrates: 4g

Protein: 2g Fat: 6g Saturated Fat: 3g Cholesterol: 17mg Sodium: 118mg Potassium: 20mg Fiber: 2g Sugar: 1g Vitamin A: 190IU Calcium: 48mg Iron: 1mg

47. KETO EGGNOG CHAFFLE

Prep Time 10 minutes

Cook Time 5 minutes

Total Time 15 minutes

Servings 2 people

Ingredients

- Chaffle
- 1/2 cup of mozzarella cheese shredded
- 1-ounce cream cheese
- tbsp Swerve confectioner's sugar substitute
- 2 tbsp almond flour
- 1/4 tsp nutmeg
- 1/8 tsp cinnamon
- 1/8 tsp ground cloves
- 1/2 tsp baking powder
- 1/2 tsp vanilla extract
- 2 tbsp heavy whipping cream

- 1 egg

Whipped Topping

- 1/4 cup of heavy whipping cream
- tbsp Swerve confectioner's sugar substitute
- 1/2 tsp vanilla extract
- 1 pinch cinnamon, nutmeg, cloves as needed

Instructions

1. Warm up the tiny waffle maker.
2. Mix the cream cheese and mozzarella cheese in a microwave-safe bowl. Heat for 30 seconds at a time until the cheeses are melted and properly blended.
3. In a mixing bowl, mix the cheese mixture, almond flour, swerve sugar replacement, baking powder, nutmeg, cloves, and cinnamon. Use your hands to knead the items until completely mixed.
4. In the same bowl as the dough, mix the egg, 2 tbsp heavy whipping cream, 12 tsp vanilla essence, and beat on high until a batter forms.
5. Place 13 of the batter in the waffle maker and fry for 3-5 minutes, or until done to your taste.
6. Step 5 should be repeated twice more to make a total of 3 chaffles.
7. In a mixing bowl, add all the whipped topping ingredients and beat on high until soft to firm peaks form.
8. Serve the chaffles with the whipped topping.

48. COCONUT CHOCOLATE CHIP MACADAMIA NUT CHAFFLES

Prep Time: 1 minute cook

Time: 9 minutes

Total Time: 10 minutes

Servings: 3 waffles

Calories: 281kcal

Ingredients

- 1 tbsp Coconut Flour
- 1/2 Cup of Roasted Macadamia Nuts
- tbsp Monkfruit
- 1/2 tsp Baking Powder
- 2 Egg room temp
- 2 ounces Cream Cheese room temp
- 1 tsp Vanilla Extract
- 1 tbsp Low Carb Chocolate Chips

Instructions

1. Collect all of the components. Submerge the egg in warm water for three-five minutes for rapid room temperature eggs. Take the quantity needed for rapid room temperature cream cheese and microwave for 10-15 seconds.
2. Preheat the Dash Mini Waffle Maker.
3. In a high-powered blender, combine Coconut Flour, Roasted Macadamia Nuts, Monkfruit, and Baking Powder until well blended. Scrape the blender's sides using a spatula.

4. In the blender, mix the egg, cream cheese, and vanilla extract. Mix on high for 10-20 seconds, or until a smooth batter is achieved.
5. Pour batter into waffle maker, top with 5-10 Low Carb Chocolate Chips, and cook for 3-4 minutes, or until the desired browning. Serve with your favorite sugar-free syrup or on its own!

Nutrition

Calories: 281kcal | Carbohydrates: 6g | Protein: 7g | Fat: 27g | Saturated Fat: 8g | Trans Fat: 1g | Cholesterol: 130mg | Sodium: 179mg | Potassium: 151mg | Fiber: 3g | Sugar: 2g | Vitamin A: 412IU | Vitamin C: 1mg | Calcium: 93mg | Iron: 2mg

49. COCONUT CREAM CAKE CHAFFLE

Servings 6 servings

Calories 157 kcal

INGREDIENTS
Chaffles:

- eggs
- 1-ounce cream cheese softened to room temperature
- 2 tbsp finely shredded unsweetened coconut
- 2 tbsp powdered sweetener blend such as Swerve or Lakanto
- 1 tbsp melted butter or coconut oil
- 1/2 tsp coconut extract
- 1/2 tsp vanilla extract

Filling:

- 1/3 cup of coconut milk
- 1/3 cup of unsweetened almond
- eggs yolks
- 2 tbsp powdered sweetener blend such as Swerve or Lakanto
- 1/4 tsp xanthan gum
- 2 tsp butter
- Pinch of salt
- 1/4 cup of finely unsweetened shredded coconut

instructions

1. Mini Dash waffle iron should be heated all the way through.

2. Stir together all of the chaffle's components in a small bowl until smooth.

3. Cook until golden brown and the waffle iron no longer steams, about 5 minutes after adding a heaping 2 tablespoons of batter to the waffle iron.

4. To produce four chaffles, repeat the process three times. There are only 3 ingredients in the recipe.

For the filling:

In a small saucepan, warm the coconut and almond milks until just steaming. It should be hot enough to make you steam, but not so hot that you boil.

Egg yolks should be softly beaten in a small bowl until pale and creamy in texture. The egg yolks should be softly drizzled into the milk while whisking it continually.

Stir regularly while the mixture heats up to a little thickening. Don't put the water on the stove to a boil. Add the sweetener and mix well.

Add the xanthan gum in a slow, steady stream while whisking continually. Cook for a further one minute, stirring occasionally.

Cook for another a minute or two, stirring constantly.

Refrigerate until cold, then pour coconut cream filling into a jar and cover with plastic wrap. The plastic wrap protects the filler from developing a skin. Cooling causes the mixture to thicken.

50. BLUEBERRY CINNAMON KETO CHAFFLES

Prep time 3 minutes

Cook time 10 minutes

Total time 13 minutes

Ingredients

- 1 cup of shredded mozzarella cheese
- tbsp almond flour
- 2 eggs
- 2 tsp Swerve or granulated sweetener of choice
- 1 tsp of cinnamon
- 1/2 tsp baking powder
- 1/2 cup of fresh blueberries
- 1/2 tsp of powdered Swerve (optional)

Instructions

1. Begin by preheating the waffle maker.
2. Begin by mixing the mozzarella cheese, almond flour, eggs, sweetener, cinnamon, baking powder, and vanilla extract.
3. When all the components have been thoroughly mixed and adequately blended, carefully fold in the blueberries. The additional moisture from frozen blueberries will make it difficult for the chaffles to crisp up.
4. Pour 1/4 to 1/3 of the butter into each waffle form, depending on the Size of your waffle maker. Allow them to cook with the cover closed.
5. Start monitoring the chaffles after around 8 minutes of cooking time. Open the waffle maker with care. If the chaffles begin to separate, shut the lid and simmer for another minute or two. A waffle maker has finished making chaffles when they are crisp and easy to open.

To prepare the chaffles:

Sprinkle some powdered Swerve on top of the chaffles. Drizzle with your preferred sugar-free, keto-friendly syrup and serve.

Nutrition

Yield 3

Serving Size 1

Amount Per Serving Calories 193 Total Fat 12g Sodium 325mg Carbohydrates 9g Net Carbohydrates 3g Fiber 2g Sugar Alcohols 4g Protein 13g

51. WAFFLE CEREAL

Prep Time: 5 mins

Cook Time: 20 mins

Total Time: 25 mins

Servings: 2

Calories: 191 kcal

Ingredients

- your favorite waffle batter OR use my paleo waffle recipe below

For paleo waffle recipe:

- large eggs
- 2 tbsp almond butter OR nut or seed butter of your choice
- tbsp coconut sugar OR granular sweetener of choice
- 2 tbsp unsweetened almond milk
- 1/8 tsp apple cider vinegar, optional - helps give the waffles that fluffy buttermilk texture
- 1 tsp maple extract OR vanilla extract
- 1 cup of superfine blanched almond flour
- 2 tbsp coconut flour
- 1.5 tsp baking powder
- 1 tsp ground cinnamon, leave out if you prefer
- waffle maker

Serve with low carb toppings of your choice:

- Sugar-free syrup, plus berries or grass-fed butter

Instructions

1. Make your favorite waffle batter according to the package directions or use the methods below.

To make my paleo waffle butter:

2. Beat the eggs or egg yolks** in a large mixing basin, then whisk in the almond butter, sugar, milk, apple cider (if using), and maple or vanilla extract.
3. Mix the almond flour, coconut flour, baking powder, and cinnamon in a mixing bowl. DO NOT OVERMIX. Mix until smooth and barely mixed.
4. Allow the batter to thicken for 3-5 minutes while the waffle machine heats up. This permits the baking powder to become active.

MAKE THE WAFFLE CEREAL

1. Preheat the waffle machine and liberally coat with pure coconut oil spray (or olive oil spray).
2. Fill your waffle oven with one or two 1 tbsp dollops, leaving enough space between them. Cook until the waffle light goes green, then close the lid (about 4-5 minutes depending on your waffle maker). Allow for 15 seconds before transferring the crispy waffles to a platter.
3. Rep with the remaining batter.
4. Serve with your preferred toppings and sides, such as milk, melted butter, low-carb syrup, or fresh berries.

Nutrition Facts

Waffle Cereal

Amount Per Serving (1 g)

Calories 191 Calories from Fat 144

Fat 16g

Carbohydrates 7g

Fiber 4g

Sugar 1g

Protein 9g

52. KETO EGGNOG CHAFFLES

Prep Time 2 minutes

Cook Time 3 minutes

Total Time 5 minutes

Servings 1

Calories 372kcal

Ingredients
For eggnog chaffles

- 1 egg
- 1 ounces cream cheese
- ¼ cup of eggnog keto
- tbsp coconut flour
- 2 tsp monk fruit
- ½ tsp baking powder
- ¼ tsp rum extract
- pinch of salt & nutmeg

For eggnog creme

- ¼ cup of heavy whipping cream
- ¼ cup of egg nog keto
- tsp erythritol powdered
- ¼ tsp rum extract
- pinch of nutmeg

Instructions

1. Preheat the waffle machine to medium heat and combine all of the ingredients for the eggnog chaffles.
2. Pour the eggnog chaffles batter into the waffle maker's middle. COOK, COVERED, FOR 3-5 MINUTES, OR UNTIL PLEASANTLY GOLDEN BROWN.
3. To make the crème, place whipping cream in a mixing basin and stir until frothy. Now, combine the remaining creme ingredients and whisk until smooth and creamy. Finally, add the nutmeg, and you're done.
4. Pour this crème over the soft eggnog and top with a sprinkling of nutmeg powder for a keto Christmas meal.

53. KETO BLACK FOREST CHAFFLE

Prep Time: 20m

Cook Time: 12m

Total Time: 30m

Ingredients
Chaffle Batter:

- eggs
- 2 ounces cream cheese, softened
- ¼ cup of almond flour

- ¼ cup of ChocZero Dark Chocolate Baking Chips, melted
- 2 tsp sweetener of your choice
- 1 tsp vanilla extract

Whipped Topping:

- 1 cup of heavy cream
- ¼ cup of ChocZero Vanilla Syrup
- tsp cherry extract

Directions

1. Mix the eggs, cream cheese, almond flour, melted ChocZero Dark Chocolate Baking Chips, sweetener, and vanilla extract in a small mixing bowl. Using an electric mixer, mix all of the ingredients.
2. Pour a tiny quantity into a small waffle machine and cook for 2-3 minutes, or until the waffle is set. Use the rest of the cake batter to repeat the above step.
3. In a medium mixing bowl, mix heavy cream and cherries to produce the cherry whipped topping. The cream should be beat with an electric mixer until soft peaks form. Mix the ChocZero Vanilla Syrup and cherry essence in a mixing bowl. Whip the mixture until firm peaks form.
4. Assemble the cake layers by sprinkling icing in between and around the cake.

54. HAM & CHEDDAR CHAFFLES

Servings 2

Prep time 5 min

Total time 10 min

INGREDIENTS

- 1 (8 ounces) package Jones Dairy Farm Ham Slices, diced
- 1 cup of shredded cheddar cheese
- 1/2 cup of almond flour
- 1/2 tsp baking powder
- eggs
- Salt and pepper, as need

DIRECTIONS

1. Preheat a waffle maker.
2. In a medium mixing bowl, mix the cheese, almond flour, and baking powder. Mix in the egg until it is entirely mixed—season with salt and pepper as need. Mix in the diced ham until it is equally distributed.
3. Spray both the top and lower molds with nonstick cooking spray once the waffle iron is heated. Scoop 14 cups to 12 cups of the ingredients into each waffle mold. Take care not to overfill. Close the top and cook for two-three minutes, depending on how crispy you prefer your chaffles.
4. This recipe yields 3-4 large chaffles or 8 small chaffles

5. To serve, cut a shape out of each ham slice with a cookie cutter. Then, in the chaffles, use all of the remaining pieces chopped up. With the ham cutouts, serve the chaffles.

55.CHAFFLES WITH BACON

Prep Time 10 minutes

Cook Time 15 minutes

Servings 2

Ingredients

- rashers of bacon
- 2 eggs
- 1 cup of grated soft melting cheese,
- 2-3 tsp grated parmesan
- 1/8-1/4 tsp black pepper
- vegetable spray for the waffle iron
- honey or maple syrup for drizzling

Instructions

1. Make little 1/6-1/4 inch cubes out of the bacon. The vegetables should be sautéed over a medium heat in a pan. REMOVE TO A PAPER TOWEL-LINED PLATTER WHEN CRISP. ALLOW IT TO COOL SOMEWHAT WHILE YOU FINISH THE REMAINDER OF THE BATTER.
2. Preheat the waffle maker.
3. In a medium mixing basin, whisk together the eggs.
4. Mix in the cheeses well. Combine the bacon lardons AND PEPPER IN A MIXING BOWL. Instead of adding salt, I use

cheese and bacon, both of which have a good amount of salt already.
5. Spritz the waffle maker. Assembling half of the battery and closing the top off. It will expand out to fill all of the iron pockets. Allow it to finish cooking. I turned it up to a higher level simply to crisp up the outside. You can pull up towards the finish to check whether it suits you. Transfer to a plate.
6. The second one will most likely not require any spray at all.
7. Serve with maple syrup or honey on the side. For a nice breakfast, you may even sprinkle with icing sugar.

56. KETO PIZZA CHAFFLES

yield: 2 mini pizzas

prep time: 3 minutes

cook time: 7 minutes

total time: 10 minutes

INGREDIENTS
Chaffle Crust

- 1 egg
- 1/2 cup of mozzarella cheese, shredded
- 1/2 tsp Italian Herb blend
- pinch garlic powder

Pizza Toppings

- tbsp tomato sauce
- 1/2 cup of mozzarella cheese, shredded
- pepperoni (optional)

INSTRUCTIONS

1. preheating the waffle maker in accordance with the manufacturer's recommendations. Preheat the oven to 400 degrees Fahrenheit.
2. mix the egg, cheddar cheese, garlic, and herbs in a small mixing bowl. Stir until everything is thoroughly blended.
3. Pour one-half of the waffle batter into the waffle maker if using a tiny waffle maker. (For a big Belgian waffle maker, use all of the butter.)
4. 3-4 minutes, or until golden brown. Rep with the other half of the batter.
5. Toppings for the chaffle crusts include tomato sauce, cheese, and pepperoni—place on a small baking sheet and 5 minutes in the oven, or until the cheese is melted

and the crust is golden.

Nutrition

YIELD: 2 SERVING SIZE: 2

Amount Per Serving: CALORIES: 238TOTAL FAT: 18gSATURATED FAT: 9gTRANS FAT: 0gUNSATURATED FAT: 7gCHOLESTEROL: 143mgSODIUM: 554mgCARBOHYDRATES: 2gFIBER: 0gSUGAR: 1gPROTEIN: 17g

57. VINTAGE CHEESE & POPPY SEEDS BISCUITS

Prep Time:5 mins

Cooking Time:15 mins

Serves:15 biscuits

Ingredients

- 100g Mainland Natural Butter, cut into cubes
- 1 1/3 cups of flour
- 1 ½ cups of grated Mainland Vintage Cheese
- ½ tsp celery salt or seasoning
- Pinch smoked paprika
- tsp poppy seeds
- 1-2 tbsp hot water

Method

1. Combine the butter and flour in a food processor and pulse until the mixture resembles medium breadcrumbs.
2. Whizz in the vintage cheese, celery salt, paprika, and poppy seeds until fully combined and starting to clump. When quickly processed again, add enough hot water to make a softball.
3. Place the dough on a floured work area and shape it into a log, rolling and shaping the ends. About 22 cm long and 5 cm in diameter.

4. Wrap in cling film and place in the refrigerator for at least 30 minutes, or until ready to cook and serve.
5. Preheat the oven to 180 degree and cut the biscuit roll into half-cm slices, arranging them on a baking pan coated with baking paper.
6. Cook for 12-15 minutes, or until the top is brown. To transfer to an airtight container, let it cool and crisp on the tray.

58. BROCCOLI AND CHEESE CHAFFLE

Prep Time: 2 minutes

Cook Time: 8 minutes

Servings: 2 chaffles

Ingredients

- 1/2 cup of cheddar cheese
- 1/4 cup of fresh chopped broccoli
- 1 egg
- 1/4 tsp garlic powder
- 1 tbsp almond flour

Instructions

1. In a mixing dish, combine the almond flour, cheddar cheese, egg, and garlic powder. With a fork, I can more easily mix everything.

2. Half of the Broccoli and Cheese Chaffle batter should be added to the Dish Mini waffle maker at a time. In a waffle machine, cook the chaffle batter for 4 minutes.

3. Allow each chaffle to firm up for 1-2 minutes on a platter. Serve alone or with sour cream or ranch dressing.

Nutrition

Serving: 1g | Calories: 170kcal | Carbohydrates: 2g | Protein: 11g | Fat: 13g | Saturated Fat: 7g | Cholesterol: 112mg | Sodium: 211mg | Potassium: 94mg | Fiber: 1g | Sugar: 1g | Vitamin A: 473IU | Vitamin C: 10mg | Calcium: 229mg | Iron: 1mg

59. AVOCADO TOAST CHAFFLE

Servings 2 servings

Calories 172 kcal

INGREDIENTS

- 1/2 cup of mozzarella cheese shredded
- 1 egg
- Pinch of salt
- 1/2 avocado mashed into guacamole and spread over the chaffle

INSTRUCTIONS

1. Preheat the tiny waffle maker. The Dash tiny waffle iron is what we use.
2. Whip the egg in a small basin.
3. Mix in the other ingredients until well blended.
4. Add half of the mixture to the tiny waffle machine and cook for 3 to 4 minutes, or until golden brown.
5. Enjoy when still warm.

NUTRITION

Serving: 1chaffle Calories: 172kcal Carbohydrates: 6.1g Protein: 13.2g Fat: 11.2g Fiber: 4.4g Sugar: 0.7g

60. BROCCOLI CHEDDAR CHAFFLE

Yield: 1 serving

Serving Size: full recipe

Prep Time: 3 min

Cook Time: 4 min

Ingredients:

- ½ cup of shredded goat's milk cheddar or regular cheddar cheese
- 1 egg
- 1-2 chopped broccolini florets,
- 1 tbsp almond flour
- Pinch garlic powder
- Pinch onion powder

Method:

1. In a medium mixing basin, mix everything with a fork.
2. Fill a waffle maker halfway with batter or a tiny waffle maker halfway with batter—Cook for about 4 minutes before removing.
3. Allow the chaffle to firm up for 1-2 minutes on a platter.

Nutrition Information:

Calories: 352| Protein: 23g | Fat: 27g | Carbs: 6g | Fiber: 1g | Net Carbs: 5g

61. LOW CARB BAGEL CHAFFLE

Yield 2 bagels

Prep time 5 minutes

Cook time 6 minutes

Total time 11 minutes

Ingredients

- 1 large egg
- 1 tsp coconut flour
- 1 tsp Everything Bagel seasoning (plus more, for Serving)
- 1/2 cups of freshly grated mozzarella cheese
- tbsp cream cheese, for Serving

Instructions

1. Preheat your tiny waffle iron by plugging it in.
2. Mix the egg, coconut flour, and bagel seasoning in a mixing bowl until thoroughly blended. Add the cheese and mix well.
3. Cook for 3 minutes with half of the egg mixture in the waffle iron.
4. Repeat with the remaining egg mixture and waffle.
5. Spread cream cheese on each bagel waffle and top with extra bagel seasoning, if desired.

Nutrition Information:

YIELD: 1 SERVING SIZE: 2 bagel waffles

Amount Per Serving:

Calories: 322 Total

Fat: 23g Saturated

Fat: 12g Trans Fat: 0g Unsaturated Fat: 8g Cholesterol: 241mg Sodium: 850mg Carbohydrates: 5gNet Carbohydrates: 4g Fiber: 1g Sugar: 1g Sugar Alcohols: 0g Protein: 19g

62. BROWN BUTTER BLUEBERRY-BACON WAFFLES

Prep time 15 mins

Cook time 20 mins

Total time 35 mins

Servings 4

Calories 524 kcal

INGREDIENTS

- strips applewood smoked bacon
- large eggs
- 1 cup of milk (whole, low-fat or non-fat OK -- I used low fat)
- tsp pure vanilla extract
- tbsp granulated sugar
- ½ tsp salt
- 1⅓ cups of all-purpose flour (or gluten-free all-purpose flour -- a brand that's 1-to-1)
- 1 tbsp baking powder

- ⅓ cup of brown butter (click here for How to Brown Butter), melted
- 1 cup of fresh or frozen blueberries
- 1 tbsp unsalted butter for the waffle iron

INSTRUCTIONS

1. A sauté pan over medium heat is sufficient for browning and crisping the bacon strips. Fill a platter with paper towels and place them in a drinking tub. Make bite-sized pieces of the crumbled tortillas.
2. Set your waffle iron to medium heat and whisk together the eggs, milk, vanilla, sugar, and salt in a medium mixing bowl. Whisk the mixture until it's completely smooth.
3. When you're ready to add the flour and baking powder, simply whisk it in until it's just combined.
4. Add the melted brown butter and mix well.
5. Add the blueberries and bacon crumbles now and combine well.
6. You may use your waffle iron to cook your batter by following the manufacturer's directions. (If your iron isn't nonstick, spray it with unsalted butter after each time you add batter to keep it from sticking.)
7. Serve the waffles when they've had time to cool on a cooling rack.

63. KETO TACO CHAFFLE

Prep Time 5 mins

Cook Time 8 mins

Servings: 1

Calories: 258kcal

Ingredients

- 1 egg white
- 1/4 cup of Monterey jack cheese, shredded (packed tightly)
- 1/4 cup of sharp cheddar cheese, shredded (packed tightly)
- 3/4 tsp water
- 1 tsp coconut flour
- 1/4 tsp baking powder
- 1/8 tsp chili powder
- pinch of salt

Instructions

1. Once it is heated, lightly oil the Dash Mini Waffle Maker.
2. Before serving, thoroughly mix all of the ingredients in a large bowl.
3. Close the cover of the waffle maker after spooning out half of the batter. Count down 4 minutes, and don't open the lid again until the timer goes off. If you do this, the taco chaffle shell will appear to be messed up, but it will be OK. Before placing the lid, let it cook for the entire 4 minutes.

4. Set aside the taco chaffle shell after removing it from the waffle iron. With the remaining chaffle batter, use the same procedure as before.
5. Set the taco chaffle shells between the cups of a muffin pan to form a taco shell on the other side. Permit to sit for a few minutes to allow flavors to mingle.
6. To consume, top tacos with the Best Taco Meat or any other dish of your choosing.
7. Toppings of your choice go great with this crispy keto taco chaffle shell.

Nutrition

Serving: 2g | Calories: 258kcal | Carbohydrates: 4g | Protein: 18g | Fat: 19g | Fiber: 2g | Sugar: 1g

64. CHICKEN BACON RANCH CHAFFLE

Prep Time: 3 minutes

Cook Time: 8 minutes

Servings: 2

Ingredients

- 1 egg
- 1/3 cup of cooked chicken diced
- 1 piece bacon cooked and crumbled
- 1/3 cup of shredded cheddar jack cheese
- 1 tsp powdered ranch dressing

Instructions

1. Set your Dash tiny waffle maker to the "heat" position.

2. Mix the egg, ranch dressing, and Monterey Jack cheese in a small bowl.
3. Then, mix with the bacon and chicken until everything is well-combined.
4. Cook for 3-4 minutes with half of the batter in your little waffle machine. The second chaffle is made by cooking the remaining batter.
5. Wait two minutes before removing it from the pan.
6. Serve with ranch or sour cream, or eat plain.

Nutrition

Serving: 1g | Calories: 200kcal | Carbohydrates: 2g | Protein: 16g | Fat: 14g | Saturated Fat: 6g | Cholesterol: 129mg | Sodium: 463mg | Potassium: 130mg | Sugar: 1g | Vitamin A: 308IU | Calcium: 148mg | Iron: 1mg

65. JALAPENO POPPER CHAFFLE

yield: 5-6 mini

prep time: 5 minutes

cook time: 5 minutes

total time: 10 minutes

Ingredients

- tbsp coconut flour
- 1 tsp baking powder
- ¼ tsp Himalayan pink salt
- slices bacon

- large eggs
- 2-3 jalapeno peppers
- 8-ounces cream cheese
- 1 cup of sharp cheddar cheese, shredded

Instructions

1. Jalapeno peppers should be washed, dried, and seeded before use.
2. One should be diced, and the others should be sliced.
3. Bacon, browned in a scissor till crisp in a mixer set at medium heat.
4. Flour, baking powder, and salt should be whisked together in a small mixing basin.
5. Cream cheese should be beaten until it is light and frothy in a mixing basin.
6. Spray generously with low-carb nonstick spray and preheat waffle maker.
7. Egg should be added to a large mixing bowl and beaten until frothy.
8. Beat in the 12 cups of cream cheese and the shredded cheese until thoroughly blended before adding the other ingredients.
9. Stir in the dry ingredients and continue beating until well blended.
10. Add the diced jalapeño and combine well.
11. Use a medium-high heat setting on a waffle maker and cook batter until it starts browning.
12. It takes around five minutes to walk outdoors.

13. Remove from heat and top with the remaining cream cheese, jalapeño slices, and crumbled blue cheese. Cool slightly.
14. Slices of bacon
15. Prepare the dish and serve it to your guests.

66. SPINACH AND ARTICHOKE CHICKEN CHAFFLE

Prep Time: 3 minutes

Cook Time: 8 minutes

Servings: 2

Ingredients

- 1/3 cup of cooked diced chicken
- 1/3 cup of cooked spinach chopped
- 1/3 cup of marinated artichokes chopped
- 1/3 cup of shredded mozzarella cheese
- 1 ounce softened cream cheese
- 1/4 tsp garlic powder
- 1 egg

Instructions

1. Set your Dash tiny waffle maker to the "heat" position.
2. Make an omelet by whisking together the eggs, garlic powder, cream cheese, and Mozzarella Cheese in a small bowl until smooth.
3. Toss in the spinach, artichokes, and chicken, then serve.

4. Cook for 4 minutes using a third of the batter in your little waffle machine. If they're not entirely done, cook for an additional 2 minutes. Make a second chaffle with the remaining batter before cooking the third.
5. Set aside for two minutes after cooking in the pan.
6. Serve with ranch or sour cream, or eat plain.

Nutrition

Serving: 1g | Calories: 172kcal | Carbohydrates: 3g | Protein: 11g | Fat: 13g | Saturated Fat: 6g | Cholesterol: 46mg | Sodium: 322mg | Potassium: 140mg | Fiber: 1g | Sugar: 1g | Vitamin A: 1119IU | Vitamin C: 8mg | Calcium: 115mg | Iron: 1mg

67. KETO BUFFALO CHICKEN CHAFFLES

yield: 4

prep time: 5 minutes

cook time: 4 minutes

total time: 9 minute

Ingredients

- ¼ cup of almond flour
- 1 tsp baking powder
- large eggs
- ½ cup of chicken, shredded
- ¾ cup of sharp cheddar cheese, shredded
- ¼ cup of mozzarella cheese, shredded
- ¼ cup of Frank's Red Hot Sauce + optional 1 tbsp for topping
- ¼ cup of feta cheese, crumbled

- ¼ cup of celery, diced

Instructions

1. Set aside a small mixing bowl with the almond flour and baking powder.
2. Low carb nonstick spray the waffle machine once it has been preheated to medium/high heat.
3. Make the eggs foamy by whisking them well in a large bowl. Beat in the spicy sauce until everything is well-combined before adding it back in.
4. Make a slurry by combining the flour mixture with the eggs and stirring until they are barely mixed.
5. Mix in the shredded cheeses until everything is well-combined before adding it back in.
6. Add the shredded chicken and combine well.
7. Cook the chaffles until they are golden brown on the outside in a preheated waffle maker. It took around four minutes.
8. Repeat Step 7 until all the batter has been used up, then remove from the waffle machine.
9. Distribute chaffles on plates and serve with feta, celery, and spicy sauce.

Nutrition Information: YIELD: 4 SERVING SIZE: 1

Amount Per Serving: CALORIES: 337TOTAL FAT: 26gsaturated FAT: 12gtrans FAT: 1gunsaturated FAT: 11gcholesterol: 165mgsodium: 958mg carbohydrates: 4gnet carbohydrates: 0gfiber: 1gsugar: 1gsugar ALCOHOLS: 0gprotein: 22g

68. BACON, EGG, AND CHEESE CHAFFLE

Prep Time 10 minutes

Cook Time 10 minutes

Total Time 20 minutes

Servings 2 people

Calories 310 kcal

Ingredients
Chaffle

- 1/2 cup of Mozzarella Cheese shredded
- 1 Egg
- tbsp Bacon crumbled

Toppings

- tbsp Cheddar Cheese shredded
- 1 tbsp Bacon crumbled
- 2 tbsp Green Onions chopped

Instructions

1. Set the tiny waffle machine to "warm" before using it.
2. Combine all of the chaffle's components in a large mixing bowl and stir until thoroughly blended.
3. Mini waffles may be made by putting half of the chaffle mixture into the maker and cooking it until it's done to your taste.
4. Add the remaining batter to the waffle maker once the first chaffle has been removed. Cook until desired doneness is reached and then remove from heat.

5. Before serving, sprinkle the chaffles with the shredded cheddar cheese, bacon crumbles, green onions and serve immediately.

69. KETO CAPRESE CHAFFLE RECIPE

Prep time: 5 minutes

Cook time: 3 minutes

Total time: 8 minutes

Servings: 1

INGREDIENTS

- 1 large egg
- 1 cup of grated mozzarella cheese
- tbsp diced tomato
- 1-2 tbsp chopped basil
- 1 tbsp almond flour
- balsamic glaze (optional)

INSTRUCTIONS

1. The waffle maker's temperature should be set correctly before you begin to prepare the batter.
2. With a fork, combine the egg and mozzarella in a bowl.
3. Lightly fold in the tomato, basil, and flour after they've been added.
4. Place the heated waffle maker's lid on top of the batter and cook the mixture according to the manufacturer's instructions.
5. About 3 minutes should do it, or until crispy and golden.
6. As soon as the meat is done, season it with salt and black pepper.

7. Remove from the heat and serve immediately. If preferred, top with more basil and balsamic glaze.

70. ARBY'S CHAFFLE

Yield 1 sandwich

Prep time 15 minutes

Cook time 10 minutes

Total time 25 minutes

Ingredients

- **For the beef:**

- 1/2 cup of beef broth
- ounces thin-sliced deli roast beef

For the chaffle bun:

- 1 egg, beaten
- 1 tsp coconut flour
- 1/4 tsp baking powder
- 1/2 cup of finely shredded mozzarella

For the low carb Arby's sauce:

- 1 tbsp sugar-free ketchup
- tsp Italian salad dressing
- 1/4 tsp Worcestershire sauce
- 1/4 tsp cracked pepper
-

Instructions
For the beef:

1. In a medium-sized saucepan, bring the beef broth to a boil. Then add the meat and let it sit for 5 minutes on low to allow the flavors to meld. While you're making the chaffle, cover and set it away.

For the chaffle:

2. The waffle maker will heat up faster if you plug it in.
3. Combine the egg, coconut flour, and baking powder in a bowl and whisk until smooth. Add the mozzarella and mix well.
4. Half the batter should be placed in the waffle maker. Cook for 3 minutes with the waffle maker closed. Use the remaining batter and waffle iron to make more.

For the Arby's sauce:

To make the Arby's sauce, mix all ingredients in a bowl and whisk until smooth.

To assemble:

Drizzle the Arby's sauce over the steak and serve on a chaffle. Add a second chaffle on top for some height.

Prepare the food and serve it right away.

Nutrition Information:

YIELD: 1 SERVING SIZE: 1

Amount Per Serving: Calories: 386Total Fat: 20gSaturated Fat: 9gTrans Fat: 1gUnsaturated Fat: 9gCholesterol: 272mgSodium: 2152mgCarbohydrates: 8gNet Carbohydrates: 7gFiber: 1gSugar: 4gSugar Alcohols: 0gProtein: 40g

71. SAUSAGE STUFFED CHAFFLE

Prep time: 5 MIN

Cook time: 10 MIN

Portion: 8 SERVINGS

Ingredients

- eggs
- cups of shredded Cheddar cheese
- ½ cup of almond flour

Directions

1. Set waffle maker to high heat.
2. Mix 4 eggs, cheese, and almond flour in a bowl and whisk to mix.
3. Spray a nonstick cooking spray on the waffle maker's top and add 2-3 tsp of chaffle batter. Top with sausage. Close the chaffle with a couple of tablespoons of batter on top of the sausage. Continue cooking the chaffles for a further 3-4 minutes before removing them and repeating the process.

72. GARLIC PARMESAN CHAFFLE

Yield: 2

Prep time: 3 minutes

Cook time: 4 minutes

Total time: 7 minutes

Ingredients

- ½ cup of cheddar cheese
- 1 egg
- tbsp parmesan cheese (powdered)
- ½ tsp minced garlic (or powdered garlic)
- ¼ tsp sea salt

Instructions

1. Make an egg parmesan gratin with shredded cheddar, garlic, and salt.
2. mix all components with a whisk or spatula until well-combined.
3. Spray coconut oil on the tiny waffle maker before heating it.
4. The waffle maker's lid should be closed after cooking the first half of the batter. After 4 minutes of cooking, take the waffles from the waffle maker and place them on a platter.
5. Sliced green onions or anything else is welcome on top if desired. Keto sandwiches are easy to create with two chaffles.

Nutrition Information:

YIELD: 2 SERVING SIZE: 1 gram

Amount Per Serving: CALORIES: 175 UNSATURATED FAT: 0g

73. CRUNCHY SAVORY KETO ZUCCHINI CHAFFLES

Prep time 10 minutes

Cook time 10 minutes

Total time 20 minutes

Ingredients

- eggs
- 2 cups of grated zucchini (about 1 fresh small zucchini)
- 1 cup of grated cheese (any type)
- 1 tbsp minced onion
- 1-2 garlic cloves, minced
- chopped fresh dill (optional but good!)

Instructions

1. set waffle machine to low and bake the waffles
2. Toss eggs with zucchini, onions, garlic, herbs, and the majority of the cheese in a large bowl. The crispy coating can be made using the remaining cheese.
3. A teaspoon of cheese on the waffle maker would be ideal (optional)
4. 1/4 cup of the zucchini egg mixture should be placed on top of the cheese.
5. Add 1 tbsp of shredded cheese on top (optional)
6. Cook for 4-5 minutes with the lid on, or until cheese is melted and crunchy.
7. Allow cooling on a rack.

8. If necessary, add more cheese and egg/zucchini combinations to make a final batch that uses up the butter.
9. Garnish with sour cream, chives, and dill, if desired.

Nutrition Information:

YIELD: 4 SERVING SIZE: 2 waffles

Amount Per Serving: CALORIES: 170TOTAL FAT: 12g saturated FAT: 6gtrans FAT: 0g unsaturated FAT: 5gcholesterol: 121mgsodium: 224mg carbohydrates: 5gnet CARBOHYDRATES: 4gfiber: 1gsugar: 2gprotein: 11g

74. BACON JALAPENO KETO CHAFFLE

yield: 2 chaffles

prep time: 1 minute

cook time: 10 minutes

total time: 11 minutes

Ingredients

- 1 egg
- 1/2 cup of shredded mozzarella cheese
- 1 tbsp almond flour
- 1/4 tsp garlic powder
- 1/4 tsp cayenne powder
- optional salt & pepper to taste

Filling:

1/4 cup of (or 2 slices) other cheese: sharp cheddar, Colby, pepper jack, or habanero are great options

tbsp jalapenos (jar or fresh, sliced or diced - add more or less to your desired spice preference)

2 crumbled slices of bacon, (or use Hormel real crumbled bacon bits)

Instructions

1. Prepare your tiny waffle maker by heating it first.
2. Set aside the ingredients for the Filling: the bacon, jalapenos, and two cheese slices
3. Place all ingredients in a bowl and whisk until well combined. It's acceptable to mix the ingredients using a fork.
4. A small amount of batter should be poured into the waffle maker once it has heated up.
5. Make a little more than half of the prepared Filling ingredients: bacon, jalapeño, and cheese slices (1/4 cup cheese).
6. Then, using a spatula, smooth over a thin layer of batter that has been spread on top of the newly formed layer. This intermediate layer should be slightly covered.
7. Allow the micro waffle maker to cook until done by closing the cover (about 4-5 minutes).
8. To see if it's working, lift the cover off the waffle maker. It's done when it's a deep golden brown color, and the edges are easily pulled away from the meat. You may need to cook the batter for an extra minute if it's clinging to the lid.

9. At this point, remove the micro waffle maker's chaffle and place it on a plate.
10. To create another chaffle, repeat steps 1-9 with the leftover batter and ingredients.
11. Prepare the dish and serve it to your guests. Served with Ranch dressing and a squeeze of Sriracha sauce, these were fantastic!

NUTRITION INFORMATION:

SERVING SIZE: entire recipe (2 chaffles)

Amount Per Serving: CALORIES: 459TOTAL FAT: 38gTRANS FAT: 0gCARBOHYDRATES: 6gNET CARBOHYDRATES: 4gFIBER: 2gSUGAR: 0gPROTEIN: 30g

75. SALMON CHAFFLE TACOS

yield: 4

prep time: 5 minutes

cook time: 5 minutes

additional time: 5 minutes

total time: 15 minutes

Ingredients

- 6 ounces cans of salmon
- 1 cup of almond flour
- 2 eggs
- 1 tsp salt
- 1 jalapeño (diced)
- ½ red onion (diced)
- ½ cup of green onion (diced)

- 1 orange pepper (diced)
- 1 tsp minced garlic
- 1 tsp dill
- 1 lemon (juiced)
- 2 tbsp mayo
- 1 cup of matchstick carrots
- 1 tbsp Siracha Mayo
- 1 tbsp Greek yogurt
- Butter lettuce

Instructions

1. Gather ingredients and get them ready. Discard the skin from the salmon and dice the veggies (remove bones if applicable)
2. Toss the salmon with the remaining green onion and half the almond flour into a bowl—season with salt and pepper.
3. heat a griddle or waffle maker
4. Make around four to five patties (depending on the size of the waffle iron)
5. 3-4 minutes each side in a waffle iron
6. Make strips by chopping the meat into small pieces.
7. Butter lettuce "tortilla" should have a sprinkle of matchstick carrots on it.
8. Butter lettuce, carrots, and the leftover green onion go on top of the salmon chaffle strip. Greek yogurt and sriracha mayo go on the side.

Nutrition Information:

YIELD: 4 SERVING SIZE: 1

Amount Per Serving: CALORIES: 494TOTAL FAT: 35gSATURATED FAT: 5gTRANS FAT: 0gUNSATURATED FAT: 28gCHOLESTEROL: 151mgSODIUM: 868mgCARBOHYDRATES: 18gFIBER: 7gSUGAR: 7gPROTEIN: 30g

---

76. BURGER BUN CHAFFLE

Servings: 2servings

Prep time : 3 minutes

Cooking time: 5minutes

Calories 137kcal

INGREDIENTS

- 1 large egg, beaten
- 1/2 cup of shredded mozzarella
- 1 TB almond flour
- 1/4 tsp baking powder
- 1 tsp sesame seeds
- 1 Pinch of onion powder

DIRECTIONS

1. In a large bowl, mix the ingredients and thoroughly mix them.
2. Half of the batter should be poured into a tiny waffle maker (or split between two)
3. You'll know it's done when the waffle maker stops steaming after 5 minutes of cooking time.
4. Allow cooling on a wire rack.

77. PULLED PORK WITH CHAFFLE BUN

Prep time :15 mins

Cook time: 1 hour

Total time:1 hour 15 mins

Servings 4

Calories 393 kcal

INGREDIENTS

- 1 ½ pound Pork tenderloin
- 1 Can Sugar-free or diet root beer
- ⅓ C. Sugar-free BBQ sauce
- Salt and pepper as needed optional

For the chaffle bun:

- cup shredded cheddar cheese
- large eggs
- ¼ tsp. Garlic powder

INSTRUCTIONS

1. Put the pork tenderloin, diet or sugar-free root beer, and salt and pepper as needed in the Instant Pot.
2. Cook for 45 minutes on manual with the dial set to "sealing," then let the pressure naturally release for 10-15 minutes.
3. Rub 13 cups of sugar-free barbecue sauce into the drained meat and stir well.
4. Set the tiny waffle machine to "warm" before using it.
5. The cheddar cheese and eggs should be thoroughly mixed in a large mixing dish.

6. Add in the garlic powder and mix well after each addition.

7. Prepare a hot waffle machine and cook 1/8 of the ingredients till done to your taste. To produce an additional two chaffles, take the first one and continue the process seven more times.
8. chaffles should have 14 of the pork on top. To make buns, top each chaffle with one extra chaffle.
9. If preferred, garnish with finely chopped green onions before serving.

NUTRITION

Calories: 393kcalCarbohydrates: 3gProtein: 56gFat: 15g

78. CHICKEN CHEDDAR CHAFFLE SANDWICH

Prep time 10 minutes

Cook time 20 minutes

Total time 30 minutes

Ingredients

- 2- 8 ounces chicken breast, or cut of choice
- salt and pepper to taste
- Olive oil for coating the pan
- eggs
- cups cheddar cheese, shredded
- tsp almond flour
- 1 tsp baking powder
- tsp mayo

- baby dill pickles, sliced
- lettuces leave
- 8-10 tomato slices (about two tomatoes)
- Sriracha sauce, optional

Instructions
To cook the chicken breast:

1. To make the chicken breasts homogeneous in thickness, use a meat tenderizer. (Place the chicken in a single-use plastic bag to prevent cross-contamination.) Use salt and pepper as needed on the chicken before serving.
2. Oil or cooking spray a medium nonstick frying pan and pre-heat it over medium heat. Cook the chicken for 6-8 minutes, occasionally stirring, until golden brown on the bottom. Cook the opposite side until it reaches the same doneness as the first.See if the chicken has reached the desired temperature an internal temperature of 165°F with an instant-read thermometer. After the meat has finished cooking, take it from the pan and arrange it on a bowl.
3. In order to marinate the chicken, add any remaining oil or liquid from the pan to the dish. Slice thinly when cool enough to handle.

For the Chaffles

1. To get your mini-waffle iron up to temperature, simply plug it in.
2. In a mixing bowl, mix the egg, shredded cheddar cheese, almond flour, and baking powder.
3. Once the iron is hot, add a little less than 14 cups of the mixture and fry until the mixture is golden brown. Take

out and place aside. Continue with the remaining mixture and repeat the procedure.

To assemble the sandwich:

1. The interior of one sandwich should be spread with one-and-a-half tbsp of mayo. The pickle slices should be layered on top of the lettuce, which should be topped with lettuce, before the tomato slices and the chicken breast are added.
2. Spread the second chaffle with another 12 tsp of mayo, sprinkle with sriracha if desired, then top with the second chaffle. Take a bite and savor it!

Nutrition Information:

YIELD: 4

SERVING SIZE: 1 sandwich

Amount Per Serving: **CALORIES:** 614TOTAL FAT: 39gsaturated FAT: 15gtrans FAT: 1gunsaturated FAT: 21gcholesterol: 342mgsodium: 1101mgcarbohydrates: 7gfiber: 2gsugar: 3gprotein: 56g

79.KETO OKONOMIYAKI CHAFFLE

Prep Time:3 minutes

Cook Time:4 minutes

Total Time:7 minutes

Ingredients
Savory Pancake Mix

- tbsp finely chopped cabbage

- 1.5 tbsp spring onions sliced thinly-the fleshy part and green tops
- 1 extra-large egg
- ½ slice of short cut bacon cut into strips or thick ham
- ⅓ cup of shredded/grated tasty cheese
- tbsp almond meal/almond flour
- ¼ tsp baking powder
- A dash of EVOO- extra virgin olive oil
- Salt and pepper to taste

Optional additional flavoring suggestions to mix into the pancake mix

To give the batter even more flavor, add a dash of tamari.

Precook 2 tbsp of calamari/squid or octopus in advance and stir it into the batter

Low Carb Okonomi Salsa Sauce-optional as sugar-free BBQ sauce can be used as well

medium tomatoes

2 tbsp Worchestershire sauce-omit if you are avoiding due to carbs, but it will impact the flavor

tsp tamari

1 tsp Dijon mustard

¼ tsp ginger crushed

1/2- 1 tsp monk fruit blend or preferred sweetener-optional

Topping Ingredients

Japanese Kewpie mayonnaise or your preferred type of mayonnaise

Flakes of bonito

Flakes of honor or strips of nori

Okonomi Salsa low carbohydrate or sugar-free barbecue sauce.

The recipe for the salsa may be found in the appendices.

Method

1. Set your waffle maker to "warm" before using. Mix all of the chaffle's components, including the EVOO, in a small bowl.
2. Lightly spread out the chaffle ingredients to cover the bottom of the waffle pan. It's a bit thick, but it'll cook and rise just fine nonetheless.
3. Cook until the chaffle is heated through and browned on both sides, about 3-4 minutes total. Gently place in a serving dish. Take gently from the oven.

To Serve

Serve immediately. Make Low Carb Okonomi Salsa (recipe is in the recipe notes below) or use Sugar-Free BBQ Sauce and Mayonnaise for a more traditional topping. 2 to 3 tablespoons of bonito flakes go on top. You may also use nori flakes instead of wakame.

You may also try adding things like a fried egg on top, salad, veggies, or radishes, or daikon radish slices.

You may serve the basic dish with an egg on top and bacon on the side as a breakfast or simple supper without the ham or bacon.

Nutritional Information

Serving: 1chaffle without topping | Calories: 655kcal | Carbohydrates: 5g | Protein: 36g | Fat: 56g | Fiber: 1g

80. KETO PHILLY CHEESESTEAK CHAFFLE SANDWICH

Prep Time 10 minutes

Cook Time 10 minutes

Total Time 20 minutes

Servings 2 servings

Calories 401kcal

Ingredients

- 2 tbsp avocado oil
- 1/4 cup of sliced onion
- 1/2 cup of sliced mushrooms
- 1/2 cup of sliced bell peppers
- 1 pinch salt and pepper
- 1/2 pound roast beef thinly sliced
- 1/2 cup of shredded provolone cheese

Instructions

1. Prepare your chaffles in accordance with the directions on your preferred recipe book. This dish serves 4, so

gather your friends. Each dish comes with two chaffles. Place them in a separate location.
2. In a medium-sized saucepan, warm the oil more than a medium heat. The onions and mushrooms should be transparent when you add them, so sauté them for 4-5 minutes to get the best flavor.
3. Cook the peppers for another 2 minutes, or until they are soft but still crunchy.
4. Add a pinch of salt and a few grinds of black pepper to the dish.
5. Make two equal piles of meat on two chaffles by dividing them in half. Add half of the vegetables and half of the cheese to the meat before serving.
6. Remove from oven and place under broiler for 1-2 minutes or until cheese is melted. Serve with the leftover chaffle on top of each sandwich!

Nutrition

Serving: 1sandwich | Calories: 401kcal | Carbohydrates: 6g | Protein: 34g | Fat: 27g | Saturated Fat: 9g | Polyunsaturated Fat: 2g | Monounsaturated Fat: 14g | Cholesterol: 87mg | Sodium: 2019mg | Potassium: 547mg | Fiber: 1g | Sugar: 3g | Vitamin A: 1457IU | Vitamin C: 101mg | Calcium: 575mg | Iron: 3mg | Net Carbohydrates: 5g

81. TURKEY BRIE CRANBERRY CHAFFLE SANDWICH

Prep time 5 mins

Cook time 5 mins

Servings 1 person

Calories 537 kcal

INGREDIENTS

- ½ cup of mozzarella grated
- 1 medium egg beaten
- 2 tbsp almond flour

FILLING

- 2 Turkey slices
- Brie slices
- 2 tbsp Cranberry chia jam

INSTRUCTIONS

1. Wipe up any excess grease from your waffle maker before using it (I give it a light spray with olive oil)
2. Add the egg, mozzarella, and almond flour to a bowl and mix well. Once everything is fully mixed, take the bowl from the heat.
3. Spoon the butter into the center of the waffle maker, being sure to cover both halves of the waffle maker. Spoon half the mixture into a smaller waffle maker at a time if you have one.

4. Cook for 5 minutes with the cover on, or until golden and hard.
5. Removing the cooked waffles with tongs and set them aside.
6. Layer the turkey, brie, and cranberries on a chafing dish. Layout the layers any way you like. The cranberry sauce comes in last for us, but it's a personal preference.
7. Cut the second chaffle in half after placing it on top of the first.
8. The sandwich may be reheated in the microwave for 20 seconds or put back in the waffle maker to regain some of its warmth.

NUTRITION

Serving: 1sandwichCalories: 537kcalCarbohydrates: 8.6gProtein: 44gFat: 36gFiber: 4.5g

82. KETO CORNBREAD CHAFFLES

Prep time 5 mins

Cook time 5 mins

Total time 10 mins

Servings 3

INGREDIENTS

- 1 egg
- 1/4 Cup of Cheddar & Jack Cheese mixture shredded

- TB Full-Fat Mayo
- 1/8 tsp maize extract can be found in the notes
- and on the website linked above.
- 1/3 cup of almond meal, which is a finer-ground version of almond flour check out the suggestions in the following remarks and link for a good brand
- 1/2 tsp baking powder
- 1/8 tsp salt

OPTIONAL

1/2 tsp If you like a sweet cornbread, use Monk Fruit sweetener.

1 TB jalapeno or green chiles diced

Instruction

1. Preheat the Mini Dash waffle iron by connecting it to the electrical outlet. It needs to warm up for 3-5 minutes before you can use it.
2. Scramble the egg in a small mixing bowl. After you've added the corn extract, add the remaining three ingredients. To blend, give everything a good stir.
3. BEFORE SERVING, INTRODUCE THE REST OF THE INGREDIENTS AND MIX WELL.
4. Add a third of the cornbread mixture to the waffle iron when it is hot and ready to use. Cook for 4-5 minutes, depending on how crispy and dark you prefer your keto cornbread to be.
5. Take it from the oven when it's done. And place it on a dish to cool. Repeat the 4-5 minute cooking time with the other half of the leftover batter in the waffle iron.
6. The last pass with all the batter. This recipe yields three tiny keto cornbread chaffles.

7. Enjoy. For up to five days, these chaffles keep nicely in the refrigerator, packed in a Ziplock bag or container. When they're cold, you can quickly reheat them in the microwave or toaster oven.

83. SHRIMP AND AVOCADO CHAFFLE SANDWICH

Prep time 15 mins

Cook time 10 mins

Total time 25 mins

Servings 4 sandwiches

Calories 488 kcal

INGREDIENTS
Cajun Flavored Chaffle

- large eggs
- 2 cups of shredded part-skim mozzarella cheese
- 1 tsp Cajun Seasoning

Chaffle Sandwich Filling

- 1 pound raw shrimp peeled and deveined
- 1 tbsp bacon grease or avocado oil
- slices bacon cooked
- 1 large avocado sliced
- ¼ cup of thinly sliced red onion
- 1 recipe Bacon Scallion Cream Cheese Spread optional
- 1 tsp cajun seasoning

INSTRUCTIONS

1. big eggs, beaten, should be in a large bowl. Add 2 cups of the low moisture mozzarella cheese and 1 tsp of the cajun spice to the mixture and stir to mix well. Fill a micro waffle machine with 14 cups of the cheese and egg mixture. The chaffle has to be browned before moving on to the next step of cooking. Once you've used up all of the egg and cheese butter, make another batch.
2. Add shrimp to a large bowl and season with 1 tsp of cajun spice, tossing to mix. Taste and adjust the amount of salt and pepper, if necessary. Sauté the shrimp in a little bacon fat in a large pan over high heat until they are opaque. Set aside the cooked shrimp in the pan. If cooling is desired, do so now.
3. To put together a Chaffle Sandwich, follow these steps: One half of a chaffle should be covered with cream cheese and bacon scallion spread. Top the chaffle with shrimp, bacon, avocado, and red onion. Add another chaffle on top of it to provide coverage. Serve immediately.

NUTRITION

Calories: 488kcalCarbohydrates: 6.01gFat: 32.22gSodium: 1122 mgFiber: 2.6g

84. LOW CARB CREAM CHEESE CHAFFLES

Prep time 5 minutes

Cook time 5 minutes

Total time 10 minutes

INGREDIENTS

- Large Eggs
- Ounces Cream Cheese, softened
- 1 tsp Monkfruit Sweetener
- 1 tsp Vanilla Extract
- ¾ Cup of Mozzarella Cheese, shredded
- tbsp Coconut Flour
- 1 tsp Baking Powder
- ½ tsp Salt
- Optional - 1 tbsp fresh lemon zest for topping

INSTRUCTIONS

1. Low carb nonstick spray the waffle machine once it has been pre-heated to medium/high heat.
2. Pour ingredients into a large mixing basin and mix with a hand mixer or whisk until frothy.
3. Beat in the mozzarella until everything is well-combined before adding the cheese back in.
4. Then, in a another bowl, mix the flour and baking powder until thoroughly mixed.

5. Mix in the dry ingredients until they are barely mixed with the egg mixture.
6. To prepare waffles, pour the batter into a hot waffle machine and cook for 4 minutes or until it turns golden brown on the outside.
7. Waffle maker chaffles are ready after they've been removed from the machine.
8. If you'd like, sprinkle some freshly grated lemon zest on top before serving.

NUTRITION INFORMATION

Yield 4

Serving Size 1 Mini Chaffle

Amount Per Serving: Calories 238 Total Fat 19g Saturated Fat 10g Cholesterol 179mg Sodium 718mg Carbohydrates 6g Fiber 2g

85. BLT CHAFFLE RECIPE

Prep Time 5 Minutes

Cook Time 5 Minutes

Total Time 10 Minutes

Servings 1 Person

Calories 512kcal

Ingredients

- 1 Batch Chaffle Recipe
- 1 Slice Sugar-Free Bacon
- 1 Slice Large Tomato
- Slices Lettuce
- 1 Tbsp Mayonnaise

Instructions

1. Make the chaffles as directed on the package and set them aside. Keep warm by wrapping yourself with a blanket.
2. There are many ways to prepare bacon (oven, microwave, or stovetop). We like to keep things simple and microwave them for around 2-3 minutes.transfer the finished dish to a platter lined with paper towels.
3. Make a BLT Sandwich by starting with one chaffle and adding lettuce, tomato, and bacon in that sequence. Place the final chaffle on top of the sandwich and slather with mayo.
4. Enjoy it right away.

86. BROCCOLI & CHEESE CHAFFLES

Prep time 5 mins

Cook time 5 mins

Total time 10 mins

Servings 1 person

Calories 125 kcal

INGREDIENTS

- ⅓ cup of raw broccoli

- ¼ cup of shredded cheddar cheese
- 1 egg
- ½ tsp garlic powder
- ½ tsp dried minced onion
- salt and pepper, to taste
- cooking spray

INSTRUCTIONS

1. Warm-up your waffle maker by plugging it in.
2. Use a fork to break and beat 1 egg in a small bowl.
3. Toss the broccoli and cheese together with the garlic powder, onion, and seasonings.
4. If necessary, coat the waffle iron with cooking spray before adding the egg mixture. Wait until the light goes out on the waffle iron's timer before closing it.
5. Then, place the top back on and let the food cook for another cycle.
6. Finish your waffle and take it from the iron using tongs or a fork.
7. Enjoy! Add butter, sour cream, or ranch dressing to your liking.

NUTRITION

Serving: 1servingCalories: 125kcalCarbohydrates: 4gProtein: 7g Fat: 9gFiber: 1g

87. KETO COPY CAT BLOOMING ONION CHAFFLE STICKS WITH DIP

Prep time 5 minutes

Cook time 5 minutes

Total time 10 minutes

Ingredients

- eggs
- ounces shredded part skin mozzarella,
- A large slice of Vidalia or sweet onion (about 10 rings)

Dip ingredients

- tbsp mayonnaise
- 2 tsp sugar-free ketchup
- 1 tsp grated horseradish
- 1/4 tsp smoked paprika
- 1/8 tsp garlic powder
- 1/8 tsp onion powder
- 1/8 tsp dried oregano
- 4-5 drops Tabasco sauce
- As need salt and pepper

Instructions

1. Plugin the waffle maker on your Dash.
2. Make sure the eggs are fluffy and light by beating them till they are.
3. Sprinkle 1/2 ounce cheese on heated waffles when ready to serve.

4. 1/4 of the beaten egg should be poured over the cheese.
5. Place a quarter of the raw onion slices on top of the cheese and egg mixture and serve.
6. Top with a half-ounce of cheese.
7. Wait until the top of the waffle maker is crisp before closing the waffle maker.
8. Cut the chaffle into strips after removing it from the pan.
9. Make four Chaffles by repeating steps 1-8 four times.

Blooming Onion Dip: Whisk together all of the dip ingredients in a small dish until well mixed.

Nutrition Information:

YIELD: 4

SERVING SIZE: 1 Chaffle

Amount Per Serving: CALORIES: 163 TOTAL FAT: 12g SATURATED FAT: 4g UNSATURATED FAT: 6g CHOLESTEROL: 21mg CARBOHYDRATES: 3g NET CARBOHYDRATES: 3g SUGAR: 2g PROTEIN: 10g

88. CRISPY KETO CHAFFLE CHIPS

Prep time 5 minutes

Cook time 24 minutes

Total time 29 minutes

Ingredients

- 1 Cup Hard Cheese

Instructions

1. Use a cheese grater or other kitchen tools to shred your cheese.
2. Prepare to chaffle by heating your Mini Dash, Chaffle Maker to high.
3. Once it's cooked through, spoon 14 ounces of shredded cheese into the middle.
4. Before continuing, wait a few minutes for the cheese's base to melt.
5. Carefully close the cover to ensure that the cheese is spread evenly throughout the Chaffle Maker.
6. It should be easy to open and not stick after 5 minutes of heating.
7. Gently pull the whole Chaffle to release the Chaffle Maker.
8. Once the Chaffle has been withdrawn from the Maker, use a pair of scissors or a cut it into the required shapes using a knife.

Nutrition

Yield 4

Serving Size 8pcs Amount Per Serving Calories 97 Total Fat 8g Carbohydrates 0g Protein 7g

---

89. KETO FRIED PICKLES

Prep Time: 3 minutes

Cook Time: 3 minutes

Total Time: 6 minutes

Servings: 1 person

Calories: 141 kcal

Ingredients

- slices hamburger dill pickle chips
- ⅓ cup of shredded pepper jack cheese

Instructions

1. spray nonstick cooking spray in waffle machine and heat to high.
2. Place half of the shredded cheese in the waffle maker's well.
3. add slices of pickled cucumber to the top tier
4. Close the waffle maker after adding the last of the cheese. Once the cheese has hardened, do not open the container for at least 2-3 minutes.

Nutrition

Calories: 141kcal

Carbohydrates: 1g

Protein: 9g | Fat: 11g

Saturated Fat: 7g

Cholesterol: 34mg

Sodium: 237mg

Sugar: 1g

Vitamin A: 290IU

Calcium: 281mg

Iron: 1mg

90. KETO CHEESESTEAK CHAFFLE SANDWICH

Prep time 15 mins

Cook time 15 mins

Total time 30 mins

Servings 4

Calories 417 kcal

INGREDIENTS

- ounces. Cheesesteak meat
- ½ Medium onion sliced
- ½ Medium bell pepper sliced
- 1 tsp Worcestershire sauce
- Salt and pepper to taste
- 1 Your choice of cheese

For the chaffle buns:

- cup shredded mozzarella cheese
- large eggs
- ¼ tsp Garlic powder

INSTRUCTIONS

1. Ensure that a tiny waffle machine is pre-heated before you begin.

2. Whisk the eggs and mozzarella cheese together in a large mixing basin until smooth.
3. Add the garlic powder and mix well.
4. In a waffle machine, place 18 of the mixture and cook until it is done to your preference. After removing the first seven times, you'll need to make another seven batches of batter.
5. Heat a pan with the cheesesteak meat over medium-high heat. Cook for a few minutes until well-browned. Take it out and place it in a different location.
6. In the same skillet, cook the onions and peppers until they are tender.
7. Replacing the meat and vegetables in the skillet, and season with salt and pepper after stirring in the Worcestershire sauce.
8. To make a sandwich, layer the chaffles with a serving of the meat mixture, a slice of cheese, and another chaffle.
9. If you like, top with freshly chopped parsley.

NUTRITION

Calories: 417kcalCarbohydrates: 4gProtein: 26gFat: 33g

Net Carbs: 4

91. CRISPY KETO JALAPENO POPPER CHAFFLE

Prep time 5 minutes

Cook time 6 minutes

Total time 11 minutes

Ingredients

- 1 jalapeno pepper, sliced in rings
- 1 egg
- 1/4 cup of grated cheese
- tbsp cream cheese

NOTE: Double ingredients if using the full-size waffle maker

Instructions

1. Connect the mini-dash waffle maker to the power source.
2. Beat an egg and shred cheese in a food processor.
3. Waffle maker should have roughly 1 tbsp of shredded cheese on it. Half of the beaten egg should be poured in. 1 tbsp cheese and 1/2 the jalapeño rings should be placed on the tortilla. 3 minutes with the lid closed.
4. When the first chaffle is done cooking, take it from the pan and let it cool on a rack while you repeat Step 3 to produce the second chaffle.
5. Spread cream cheese on the two prepared chaffles.
6. Open-faced is best, although sandwiches also work.

Nutrition Information:

YIELD: 1

SERVING SIZE: 1

Amount Per Serving: CALORIES: 146 TOTAL FAT: 29.6g TRANS FAT: 0g CARBOHYDRATES: 3g NET CARBOHYDRATES: 3g FIBER: 0g PROTEIN: 19g

92. PEPPERONI PIZZA CHAFFLES

Ingredients

- large eggs
- 3/4 cup of shredded mozzarella cheese
- 1/4 cup of almond flour
- 1/2 tsp baking powder
- ½ tsp Italian seasoning
- 1/4 tsp garlic powder
- 3/4 cup of pepperoni, chopped

Instructions

1. The eggs should be thoroughly beaten in a large mixing basin. Using a rubber spatula, mix the remaining ingredients until well-combined.
2. Waffle makers should be heated in accordance with the manufacturer's recommendations for doing so. Be cautious not to overfill the waffle maker while adding the batter (approximately 2 scoops for the Dash waffle maker).
3. When there is no more steam coming from the machine, and the waffles are a golden brown color, remove them from the waffle maker.

4. chaffles' worth of nutrition: Nutritional information is based on one chaffle serving.

Amount Per Serving: Calories: 198 TOTAL FAT: 13.3g CHOLESTEROL: 99MG SODIUM: 509MG

CARBOHYDRATES: 2.5g NET CARBOHYDRATES: 2G FIBER:0.5g Sugar:0.5g PROTEIN:13g

93.CHAFFLE PEPPERONI PIZZAS

Prep: 15 mins

Cook: 10 mins

Total: 25 mins

Servings: 2

Yield: 2

Ingredients
Chaffle:

- ¾ cup of shredded mozzarella cheese, divided
- 1 large egg
- 1 tbsp almond flour
- ¼ tsp dried oregano
- ¼ tsp dried basil
- ¼ tsp garlic powder
- ⅛ tsp red pepper flakes

Topping:

- tbsp no-sugar-added marinara sauce
- slices pepperoni, quartered
- 1 pinch dried basil (Optional)

Directions

Step 1
Pre-heat the oven's broiler to high and place a rack approximately 6 inches from the heat source in the oven. Prepare a tiny waffle iron by heating it to 350 degrees Fahrenheit. Cover a baking sheet with aluminum foil.

Step 2
1 egg, oregano, basil, garlic powder, and red pepper flakes are mixed together in a bowl with 1/2 cup of mozzarella cheese.

Step 3
Spread out the batter with a spoon after pouring half of it onto the hot waffle iron. When heating stops and the chaffle is thoroughly toasted, 3 to 4 minutes should be enough time to close the waffle iron and cook. Repeat with the remaining batter and chaffles on the prepared baking sheet.

Step 4
Mix marinara sauce, mozzarella, pepperoni, and basil in a large bowl; divide evenly between 2 chaffles.

Step 5
Broil in the pre-heated oven for about a minute or until the cheese is melted and bubbling, being careful not to burn them.

Nutrition Facts
Per Serving:

120 calories; protein 6.1g; carbohydrates 6.1g; fat 8g; cholesterol 99.9mg; sodium 262.8mg

94. KETO CHAFFLE PULLED PORK SANDWICH WITH CREAMY COLESLAW

Servings 4

Prep time 25 minutes

Cook time 90 minutes

Calories 1000

INGREDIENTS

- 1 bone-in pork butt
- tbsp sugar-free barbecue sauce

KETO CREAMY COLESLAW

- 1 bag shredded cabbage or coleslaw mix
- 1 cup mayonnaise
- tbsp heavy cream
- 1 tsp creole mustard
- 1 tbsp erythritol
- 1 tsp cayenne pepper (optional)
- 1 tsp garlic powder
- 1 tsp coarse ground black pepper
- 1 tsp coarse ground salt

CHAFFLES

- lb. of your favorite cheese (16 slices works best)
- eggs

DIRECTIONS

1. To begin, score the roast's fat side with a sharp knife. By slicing the fat, the seasoning will be able to get deeper into the meat, resulting in a distinct texture.
2. In order to give your spices or rub a greater chance of sticking to your meat, drip in a small amount of wetness to the texture meat before applying your seasonings or rub.
3. Applying the rub on the meat and allowing it to sit for few minutes a countless period of time 15-20 minutes while you ignite yours, according to the manufacturer's recommendations.
4. The fat side of the pig butt should be down on the grate so that it protects the meat, and the fat crisps up when you rip the pork into pieces to provide flavor and texture. Smoke until the interior temperature reaches 165 degrees fahrenheit with the lid off. After that, put it back in the cooker until the internal temperature is 205 degrees.
5. Take the pan from the heat and set it aside to cool. Discard any remaining liquid in the pan and use a separate container to collect the fat. Continue pulling the pork roast into medium-sized bits, removing any big pieces of fat or tendon, and returning the juices to the pan.
6. Add a bit of additional flavor to the pulled pork by sprinkling it with the same rub you used to cook with and tossing it in the cooking fluids.
7. To make the coleslaw dressing, combine all the ingredients and season to taste. Serve with a side of cabbage (or a coleslaw mix). Initially, the coleslaw may

appear thicker, but after resting in the fridge for an hour, the consistency will normalize.
8. Mini waffle iron should be heated up before use. Sprinkle shredded cheese over the bottom of the waffle maker or place a piece of cheddar on the waffle iron. Over the melted cheese, pour half of a beaten egg. Close the waffle iron and add a piece of cheddar or shredded cheese to the gg. Allow it to fry for another three minutes (until crisp on the edges) if you like a crunchier result.
9. If you don't want to eat the chaffles, assemble a sandwich in a bowl and serve it that way.

95. TEX-MEX CHAFFLES

Prep Time 10 minutes

Cook Time 3 minutes

Total Time 13 minutes

Servings: 8

Ingredients

- large eggs
- 3/4 cup of finely diced red bell pepper
- 1 cup of finely diced sweet onion
- 1 clove garlic, minced
- scallions, diced
- 1 cup of shredded Pepper Jack cheese
- 1/2 tsp salt
- 1/2 tsp pepper
- pinch of cumin

- If preferred, top with salsa, sour cream, and chopped cilantro.

Instructions

1. Set waffle iron to medium heat and pre-heat it.
2. Whisk the eggs in a large bowl until they are light and fluffy. Then, mix with the bell pepper and onion, garlic, scallions, and cheese with salt, pepper, and cumin.
3. Non - stick cooking spray should be used to coat the waffle iron grids on both the top and bottom halves.
4. As you pour, make sure to include everything that has fallen to the bottom of the bowl in the egg mixture. Cook for two-three minutes, depending on the size of your waffle maker until the eggs are no longer liquid and the exterior is golden.
5. Take the chaffle from the grids with an offset spatula and serve on separate plates.
6. If required, continue with the remainder of the mixture.
7. Dollop on some salsa, top with some sour cream and fresh cilantro and serve right away.

Nutrition

Calories: 137kcal | Carbohydrates: 3g | Protein: 10g | Fat: 9g | Saturated Fat: 4g | Polyunsaturated Fat: 1g | Monounsaturated Fat: 3g | Trans Fat: 1g | Cholesterol: 199mg | Sodium: 295mg | Potassium: 145m g | Fiber: 1g | Sugar: 2g | Vitamin A: 847IU | Vitamin C: 19mg | Calcium: 142mg | Iron: 1mg

96. ULTIMATE KETO PROTEIN CHAFFLE

Servings 1

Prep time 5 minutes

Cooking time 5 minutes

Calories 369kcal

INGREDIENTS

- 1 scoop protein powder (25-30g)
- 50g cream cheese
- 1 medium/large egg
- tbsp cream or milk (45ml)
- 1 tsp baking powder
- Sweetener to taste

DIRECTIONS

1. Set waffle maker to pre-heat mode.
2. Add the cream cheese, egg, and cream to a mixing bowl and mix well. Make sure there are no lumps left after you've finished whisking.
3. Unflavored protein powder can be used without sweetness if desired.
4. Whisk together the baking powder and protein powder in a large bowl until smooth.

5. Pour the ingredients into the molds and close the cover of the waffle maker after it has heated up.
6. Until golden and crispy, about 5 minutes in a 400°F oven
7. Proceed in this manner until all of the butter has been utilized.
8. Serving suggestions: butter or your preferred sugar-free syrup on the waffle

97. KETO CHAFFLE CUBAN SANDWICH

Prep Time 20 minutes

Cook Time 15 minutes

Slow Cooker Time 8 hours

Total Time 8 hours 35 minutes

Servings 1

INGREDIENTS
Cuban Mojo Pork

- tbsp Olive oil (extra virgin)
- 2 tsp sea salt
- 1 tsp Pepper
- 3-pound Pork shoulder ((pork butt))
- ¼ cup of Orange juice (fresh)
- ¼ cup of Lime juice (fresh)
- 1 tbsp Cumin
- cloves Garlic (finely chopped)
- 1 ½ tsp Oregano
- ¼ tsp Red pepper flakes

Chaffle

- 1 Egg (beaten)
- ½ cup of Cheddar cheese (grated)
- 1 tbsp Almond flour (blanched)
- ¼ tsp Baking powder

Cuban Sandwich

- tbsp Butter
- ounces Ham (roasted, one slice)
- ounces Pulled pork ("mojo" seasoned and hot)
- 2 ounces Swiss cheese (two slices)

1 tbsp Mustard (stone-ground or yellow)

- slices Pickles (sandwich sliced dills)

INSTRUCTIONS
Cuban Mojo Pork

1. When using a Dutch oven or a big pot, heat the oil over high heat until it is shimmering.
2. Sear the pork on all sides after seasoning with salt and pepper. It took around ten minutes.
3. Mix the orange juice, lime juice, cumin, oregano, red pepper flakes, and garlic in the slow cooker and stir to mix. Add to slow cooker. After that, form a well in the center and add the pork, rolling it up until it is entirely coated with the batter.
4. It's fine to cook for eight hours on low heat or for six hours on high heat.

5. Pull the "mojo" pork from the roast and use it in sandwiches by separating it with two forks. You'll have plenty for a few sandwiches and some leftovers, so plan accordingly.

Chaffle

1. Heat mini-waffle maker until ready by spraying with cooking spray.
2. All the chaffle components should be mixed in a small dish. You may also use a blender to mix the ingredients.
3. Fill the waffle maker to the brim with batter and spread it out to the edges. Useless each time if you filled the first one too full to avoid spills. With the lid closed, the cooking time is three and a half minutes.
4. Then, remove the first chaffle and let it cool on a cooling rack before re-baking it.

Cuban Sandwich

1. In a small pan, heat the "mojo" pork until it is hot (about 3 minutes). To steam the cooked pork, put three tablespoons of water and a lid over a pan with butter melted in it. While the chaffles are cooking, apply stone ground mustard on one side.
2. One chaffle half should have two pieces of swiss cheese stacked on it. Finish with a few thinly sliced pickle sandwich thins and deli ham, then the spicy "mojo" pork, another piece of Swiss cheese, and a final slice of Swiss cheese. Add a second chaffle on top for some height.
3. Toss the sandwich with the melted butter in a large skillet set to medium heat. Warm the sandwich by pressing it onto a smaller cast-iron pan and letting it sit there. After

then, turn the sandwich over and re-apply pressure to the other side. It took me a total of three minutes. Another option is to warm your sandwich up on a panini or sandwich press, then top with cheese. Serve immediately after being sliced in half.

NUTRITION

Calories: 1073kcal | Carbohydrates: 12g | Protein: 64g | Fat: 85g | Saturated Fat: 45g | Cholesterol: 406mg | Sodium: 2955mg | Potassium: 1173mg | Fiber: 5g | Sugar: 6g | Calcium: 1199mg | Net Carbs: 7g

98. GARLIC AND HERB CHAFFLE

Total time 10 minute

Prep time 5 minute

Servings 1

INGREDIENTS

large egg	1
Mozzarella cheese shreds, with additional on hand to offer	2 Tbsp
½ cup almond flour	
garlic powder	½ tsp
dried oregano	½ tsp
dried parsley	½ tsp

salt 1/8 tsp

Directions

1. Spray 7-inch waffle iron with nonstick cooking spray and heat it up.
2. A medium bowl is a perfect size for whisking together the various ingredients. The batter should be cooked in the waffle iron for about 5 minutes, or until it turns a light brown color.
3. Then top with your preferred veggie toppings and any remaining mozzarella cheese, if using. Serve.

PER SERVING:

Calories   330

Total Fat   23 g

Saturated Fat 9 g

Carbohydrate 6 g

Dietary Fiber 4 g

Protein   23 g

Cholesterol   215 mg

Sodium   615 mg

99. KETO BELGIAN CHAFFLES

PREP TIME 2 mins

COOK TIME 4 mins

TOTAL TIME 6 mins

SERVINGS 2

INGREDIENTS

- large eggs
- 1.5 Cup jack & cheddar cheese shredded

INSTRUCTIONS

1. Pre-heat the waffle iron by connecting it to the wall outlet.
2. Scramble the eggs in a small dish while it's boiling up. Mix in the cheese until it's all combined.
3. Place a waffle iron on the stove and heat it to waffle-making temperature before adding the batter. The batter yields two chaffles the size of Belgian waffles. It's possible to fill every waffle cavity to the brim. However, compared to ordinary waffle batter, this batter won't expand as much.
4. Allow the waffle iron to cook for 4 minutes with the lid closed. Lift the lid and use a fork to penetrate the edge of the chaffle to lift and remove it.
5. Chaffles at 300 calories each provide 23 grams of fat, 20 grams of protein, and 2.6 grams of carbohydrates (depending on the cheese you use)

100. KETO NUTTER BUTTER CHAFFLE

Prep time 5 minutes

Cook time 5 minutes

Total time 10 minutes

Ingredients
Chaffles:

- 2 Eggs
- 1-and-a-half cups of part-skim mozzarella (2 ounces)
- 1 tbsp sweetener
- 1/2 tsp vanilla extract
- 1/4 cup of PB&Me almond powder

Nutter Butter Filling:

- 1/4 cup of almond butter
- 2 tbsp unsalted butter(softened)
- 1/4 cup of powdered sweetener
- 1/2 tsp vanilla
- pinch of salt (omit if you used salted butter)

Instructions

1. The sugar and vanilla extract should be well mixed with the eggs in a large bowl.
2. Set the waffle machine to high heat.
3. Put cheese on the bottom of the pan (1 tbsp per chaffle)
4. Pour the egg mixture over the cheese and let it sit for a few minutes (about 2 tbsp per chaffle)
5. Top with cheese if desired (1 tbsp per chaffle)

6. Cook with the lid closed until the bacon is crispy.
7. In order to finish all combinations, just keep continuing until all of the eggs and cheese have been utilized.
8. For a full-size waffle machine, you won't have to do much more than use half the cheddar, pour the egg mixture over the bottom, then sprinkle the remaining cheese over that.
9. Using a wire rack, let the chaffles cool to room temperature.

Filling:

Small bowl, bowl. Mix for the filling.

Blend until smooth using a wooden spoon.

Distribute over the chaffles in an equal layer.

Sandwich the chaffles together like a cookie sandwich.

Make stripes, squares, or any other form you like from the sheet of paper.

Nutrition Information: YIELD: 4 SERVING SIZE: 1

Amount Per Serving: CALORIES: 264 TOTAL FAT: 21g carbohydrates: 6gnet CARBOHYDRATES: 4g fiber: 2g protein: 14g

THE END

Made in the USA
Columbia, SC
02 May 2025